Our Beginning

Kay Summers McKean

Our Beginning

GENESIS
THROUGH THE EYES
OF A WOMAN

DPI
DISCIPLESHIP
PUBLICATIONS
INTERNATIONAL

One Merrill Street
Woburn, MA 01801
1-888-DPI-BOOK (374-2665) • FAX 617-937-3889

Our Beginning
©1996 by Discipleship Publications International
One Merrill Street, Woburn, MA 01801

Printed in the United States of America

Cover design: Chris Costello
Cover illustration: "Woman Seated Under the Willows" by Claude Monet (1880)
©1986 National Gallery of Art/FPG International
Interior layout: Laura Root
Photo on back cover courtesy of Kingdom News Network

ISBN 1-57782-001-0

To Mary Stripling Allison,
who was there for me in the beginning,
and who showed me the way.

Contents

Acknowledgments

Thanks to my husband and children, who have allowed their lives to be exposed on these pages, and who have supported and encouraged me in my writing. Thanks to Sam Laing, one of the first to show me how exciting the Bible could be. Thanks to my assistant Anne-Mer Slebodnick. Thanks to the "midwife" in this labor of love, my editor Sheila Jones.

Foreword

Kay McKean has been my friend for almost twenty years. I have watched her grow spiritually and emotionally through good times and hard times, faith and struggles, tears and laughter. Her commitment to the Lord and to his purpose for her life has brought her to a stage of maturity to enable her to write *Our Beginning* for us all. She lives the dedicated life she shares with us in this book.

"The Wakening," or "genesis," of our friendship was at a Christian seminar in Florida. Our friendship began with a simple introduction by our dear friends, Kip and Elena McKean. Each time we talked in the fellowship we deepened our acquaintance. Then I visited a "women's day" that Kay had organized in Columbia, South Carolina, and an even deeper relationship began. I remember meeting her in Chicago several months later, where we shared with each other that we really believed God meant for us to have a special friendship. We later became partners in the gospel in Boston and now are partners in world evangelism. Whether relaxing together or struggling for each other's growth, our relationship as sisters is ever growing. Today, our bond of unity is so strong that either of us would die for the other.

"The Wonder" of Kay's life is that her confidence truly comes from God. She is creative and orderly; she is her husband's helper and she praises God. Truly Kay is motivated by "The Woe" that paradise is lost to most people because of their sin and disobedience to God. Satan, the father of lies, tells us that sin is pleasant and that we, without God, have the answer for our lives, our pleasure, our future—but what about eternity? Have you ever been with a person who is facing death and doesn't know God?

Kay is a reliable "Witness" for God. She is now in the prime of her life. She has experienced enough of the cycle of life to have been matured by pain. She is in the midst of running the marathon for God because she realizes that "any people, any race, any culture, any nation that neglects the creator is doomed."

One of the most powerful chapters of *Our Beginning* is about our father Abraham—"The Wayfarer." The point is made that Abraham's relationship with God is the real origin of his faith. Sarah's relationship with Abraham allows her to trust and respect him even when they "take matters into their own hands." Hopefully, we can also relate to their complete respect, humility and submission to God as well as their gratitude. It is obvious from what is written that Kay has made the choice to build her faith rather than to be crushed by circumstances. She is a great example of uncompromising obedience to God.

"The Welcoming" is the love story of Isaac and Rebekah. God works through us when we are weak and when we are strong—through "thick and thin," as my grandmother used to say. Kay's depth of insight will help you to always remember this amazing real-life story.

Kay writes, "The more I know him [God], the more I know myself and the more I can be myself with others." For almost twenty years, I have watched Kay grow spiritually to the point that she can honestly make this statement. She has wrestled with God as Jacob did. Most of all, like Jacob, she has wrestled with herself. Her adventure in faith has led her to spend days and nights in prayer. From her wrestling, we can again be inspired.

Perhaps the topic that most binds Kay and me together relates to the chapter entitled "The Wait"—refusing to be a victim. We have waited and prayed for each other through hard times. Our spiritual relationship, coupled with a learner's spirit, has helped us to encourage each other not to moan, but rather to be honest, reliable, respectful, pure, grateful, trusting, loving and willing to wait for God's blessing.

We know that "this is the day that the Lord has made" and that we should "rejoice and be glad in it." We know that "in all things God works for the good of those who love him," and that he wants to bless us. We must work hard (persevere) to be with him through eternity. My highest praise to Kay for reminding me of what to do and how to do it.

I love you, Kay.

To everyone, I recommend *Our Beginning.*

Patricia Gempel
Director of Development
HOPE Worldwide

The Wakening

1

His mother planted a kiss on his cheek as he hurried out the door. His father, building a table in the yard, wiped his brow with one hand and waved with the other. As he ran down the path, the sounds of his father's pounding mallet grew softer until he was out of earshot. He caught up to a group of other boys and greeted them with a smile. Impishly, he suggested a race—who can get there first? The boys bolted, yelling and laughing, struggling to be the first to the door.

As they scuffled into the rabbi's home, hot and out of breath, the boys took on a more serious mood. It was time to learn from the honored rabbi the great teachings of their history. It was time to be trained in the law of their people. It was time to learn of their forefathers and of the plan that God had for his people. It was time to learn of their roots—nationally, racially and religiously. Jesus looked up, waiting expectantly as the rabbi began: "In the beginning..."

Surprised by Genesis

Fast forward to the year 1975. I was a recent college graduate, ready to embark on my life as a single working woman. I lived with three other young women in a little apartment in Florida. It was a hot, humid June, and I was making goals for the summer. What did I want to accomplish? How did I need to grow? I had been a Christian for less than a year, and it was an exciting time! I had a new life, forgiveness from sin, great Christian friendships, and most wonderful of all, a relationship with God. I had learned so much in the previous months—about God, about myself, about life—yet I knew I had so much more to learn.

I had grown to truly love the Scriptures by that time, and to find so much help and guidance in the word of God. For that I am eternally grateful to my early teachers. All that year, I'd read so much in the New Testament, studying the life of Christ and the letters of the apostles. I'd prayed through the Psalms, and gained wisdom through the Proverbs. In a dilemma so often faced by young Christians (and old), my question was: "What now? What should I study this summer in my quiet times?"

Someone suggested that I study the book of Genesis. But I'd read that, hadn't I? Sometime? Didn't I know the story of Adam and Eve and Noah's Ark? Didn't I know about Moses parting the Red Sea? Or at least I'd seen the movie. Oops! That's not even in Genesis? Well, maybe I didn't really know the book. Maybe I did need to study it. Maybe I needed to pray that God would reveal to me what I needed to learn from this book.

And learn I did. Every day, reading chapter after chapter of the rich history of the people of God, I was amazed with one consistent thought: Human nature hasn't changed! There I was, in the era of disco, drugs and disillusionment, and yet I could relate to people who lived long before me. Despite thousands of years of increased sophistication, medical and technical advancement, incredible industry and inventions, the one thing that had remained constant was the basic nature of people. From Adam and Eve to Joseph, I saw that men and women in the beginning of time had the same fears, hopes, dreams and weaknesses that I faced every day.

Over the past two decades, I have continued to study the book of Genesis, and I am constantly reminded of the wealth to be found in this book. Now I am a "woman of the nineties"—I have a husband, two kids, a job and a home. And the learning continues. Genesis never becomes dry to me. There's something in it for everyone of every age.

A Book for All

Why should all disciples study the book of Genesis? Jesus, our example and guide in life, was trained in Jewish history himself. Genesis, the first book of the Bible, the "beginning," is a book about God revealing himself to man. It is a book that provides fundamental teaching that is essential in order to fully understand all of the New Testament. Genesis gives us, as Christians, *our* background. It tells us of the creation and the fall of mankind, and of the promise of redemption. It helps us to understand the loving nature of God. It opens our minds to what "makes people tick."

The Gospels and epistles of the New Testament are filled with references to characters and events that are recorded in Genesis. The "Hall of Faith," found in Hebrews 11, focuses on some of the main players in the book of Genesis. Two full chapters of Galatians as well as the fourth chapter of Romans refer to Genesis. Jesus himself speaks often of circumstances and people that we would not know or understand if it were not for this book of Genesis. The list goes on and on, reminding us that Genesis is a book that we, as disciples of Jesus in this century, must study and strive to understand. And if that is not enough to convince us to study Genesis, even Paul, in Romans 15:4, states: "For everything that was written in the past was written to teach us, so that through endurance and the encouragement of the Scriptures we might have hope."

Genesis is a book that is full of excitement, adventure and drama. It deals with nature, with people, with families and with civilizations. This book exposes mankind in its sinful state more bluntly and realistically than anything you'll ever see on prime-time television. Hatred, violence, rape, revenge, betrayal and conflict are all there. Yet, in the midst of all this, we can see God's firm hand in dealing with his people—still believing in them and providing hope. As we read this book, we can learn from the good and from the bad. We can apply the never ending spiritual principles to our lives as we live in a modern era that, in many ways, is not so very different from the past.

Through a Woman's Eyes

Each time I read the book of Genesis, I read it first and foremost as a disciple who wants to learn how to follow Jesus better; who wants to learn more about God and about people so that I can be more godly and productive for him. But I also read the book as a woman, bringing my uniquely female perspective with me.

In each of the chapters of this book we will learn from God and from real-life people. By studying God's process of creation, we will learn to imitate his creativity in our lives and homes. As we study Adam and Eve we will see ourselves and our sins more clearly. The story of Noah and the flood can become less of a children's story and more of a challenging example. We can be inspired by Abraham to trust totally in God. We can see our own weaknesses and strengths as we study Rebekah. We can learn about sincerity as we take a real look at Jacob. Going through the life of Joseph will enable us to see the sovereignty of God. Each incident, each person that is revealed through the book of Genesis can teach us so much.

I offer *Our Beginning* to anyone who chooses to read it, but my thoughts are addressed specifically to women. There is so much that we, as sisters in Christ, can learn from one another! We are each different, and yet we are the same. Eve is the mother of us all. As I write this book, my desire is to pass on the guidance and help that I have received from so many wonderful Christian women. And you, the reader, must pass it on to others. In that way, we learn even more.

My prayer is that this book will enlighten you, and encourage you to fall in love with the word of God more than ever before. My goal for you, my sister, is that this book will increase your faith, help you to appreciate salvation, make God more real to you, and assure you that God can change and use you, an ordinary woman, in extraordinary ways.

· *Taking It Home* ·

1. Have you ever thought much about the fact that Jesus was Jewish? Have you realized that his heritage is now your heritage, even if you are Gentile? How much do you know about your heritage as it is mapped out in the Old Testament? How do you feel about learning more as you study this book? What do you specifically hope you will learn?

2. Women loved their children, cried when a friend died, and laughed at jokes thousands of years ago, just as they do today. Jealousy, hatred, envy, insecurity and joy all felt the same too. How does realizing this cause you to think about getting to know the people who were part of "our beginning"?

3. Had you realized that Genesis is quoted so much in the New Testament? What does this tell you about your need to know the facts and to understand the message of Genesis?

4. This book is written by a woman primarily for women. Why is it important to you to hear biblical truths from a woman's point of view?

The
Wonder

2

Genesis
1-2

In the beginning, God...

"The beginning" is not the beginning of God, but the beginning of us. God has always been here, even though we can't totally understand this truth. Surely I'm not the only one who's been stumped by the question of a young child: "Where did God come from?" Yet God never worries about proving his existence. He *is*, always *has been*, and always *will be*. As he described himself to Moses, "I am."

God's word to us, the Bible, is our source of true knowledge. In it, we find the realities of life. Although we are bombarded daily with ungodly and unbiblical ideas and theories about how we got here, the first verse of the Bible says it all: God! The Bible never claims to be exhaustive in its explanation of the intricacies of creation, but it covers enough. The purpose of the recording of creation is not for scientific understanding or even historical enlightenment, but for us to understand that God is the source of our very existence.

God Has a Plan

Before we move on to the actual creation, I want to remind you of what was going on *before* creation. Not only was God there, but Jesus was, too:

> *In the beginning was the Word, and the Word was
> with God, and the Word was God. He was with God
> in the beginning (John 1:1).*

> *"And now, Father, glorify me in your presence with
> the glory I had with you* before the world
> began...*Father, I want those you have given me to
> be with me where I am, and to see my glory, the glory
> you have given me because you loved me* before the
> creation of the world" *(John 17:5, 24, emphasis
> added).*

This first lesson of creation shows us that from the very
start, God had a plan for our lives. Nothing was done without
a purpose. God did not create the world on a whim to see
what would happen, but was prepared for all that would oc-
cur. Even from the outset, we can be secure in God's ultimate
concern and sovereignty in our lives. Paul makes this truth
clear in Ephesians 1:4:

> *For he chose us in him before the creation of the world
> to be holy and blameless in his sight.*

His plan to offer each of us salvation was in place before
he ever created a thing. How secure we should feel to know
that our Father was planning good things for us thousands of
years before we were born. With that thought, we can move
on with the rest of the story: Life begins!

And God Said

> *In the beginning God created the heavens and
> the earth. Now the earth was formless and empty,
> darkness was over the surface of the deep, and
> the Spirit of God was hovering over the waters.*

*And God said, "Let there be light," and there
was light. God saw that the light was good…"
(Genesis 1:1-4a).*

In the mid 1980s a movie came out entitled *The Never
Ending Story*. The hero was trying to stop "The Nothing" that
was taking over the world by emptying all life into a dark,
hopeless abyss. Ultimately, "The Nothing" was powerful because it was fueled by the dying dreams and hopes of man.

Genesis shows us the complete opposite: God took "the
nothing," fueled it with his dreams and created life! In the
absence of any substance or tools, from complete chaos and
nothingness, God's word changed everything, and our world
began to be shaped. Centuries later, Paul would remind the
early disciples of God's power, saying he was the one "who
gives life to the dead and calls things that are not as though
they were" (Romans 4: 17b).

At God's word, light came to be. Illumination was the first
to be created. The source was not our sun or another distant
star, for they had yet to be formed (on the fourth day), and yet
light was there. The implications are obvious. Isn't "seeing the
light" the beginning of all great things? In the Old Testament,
light was always symbolic of life and blessings. Psalm 27:1 is a
reminder that God himself is our "light and salvation," and
Psalm 97:11 states:

> *Light is shed upon the righteous
> and joy on the upright in heart.*

In the New Testament, the symbolism continues. John
says that God, himself, *is* light (1 John 1:5). Paul also reminds us in Ephesians 5:14 that light makes all things visible. God's light makes his glory "visible" to our hearts
through Christ:

> *For God, who said, "Let light shine out of darkness,"*
> *made his light shine in our hearts to give us the light*
> *of the knowledge of the glory of God in the face of*
> *Christ" (2 Corinthians 4:6).*

And so the six days of creation began, each day building on the one before. Throughout the process, God "evaluated" his handiwork: "And God saw that it was good." Everything that was made on one day would be needed on the next. There was no trace of disorder. God began with the actual earth, water and sky, then formed vegetation, the seasons and living creatures for the earth, the water and the sky. Finally, on the sixth day, God made man and woman. "And God saw that it was very good." God was pleased with what he had created.

Reading about the creation of our world makes me look out of my window in awe. As the song says, "This *is* my Father's world." The grass, the trees, the stars in the night sky are all so beautiful. We see such breathtaking sights every day and often fail to appreciate them. As disciples we should appreciate the wonders of nature more than anyone. "God richly provides us with everything for our enjoyment" (1 Timothy 6:17). God created nature for us!

More than even the beauty of this world, I'm in awe of our creator God. I have learned from these scriptures that (1) God is creative (2) God has order and a plan and (3) God is pleased with his work and confident that it is good. Now, if as disciples we are to imitate God, then it naturally follows that we will be creative; that we will have a plan for our lives; and that we can be pleased with our work and confident, because of God's grace, that it is good.

Imitating God's Character

Creativity

We can't create a universe, but we can "create" our world to follow in the dreams of God. Do you consider yourself to be creative? The word "creativity" often conjures up thoughts of being "artsy"—someone who can paint, decorate, draw, do crafts, etc. I personally could never live up to that definition. If you saw some of my artwork or even my handwriting, you would agree. But each person has been created by God with some talent, some gift, *something*. It's our responsibility to figure out what we have and find ways to use it to his glory.

This talent may not be a tangible, artistic ability that would produce something to hang on a wall, but may be some strength that, with creativity, can build up the kingdom of God. Perhaps you might become an awesome letter-writer and encourage saints all over the world. Maybe your talents lie with children; you might become a teacher that kids can't wait to see on Sunday morning. Perhaps you have figured out the key to having great friendships that can be an example to other women. Or maybe you have an effectiveness in evangelism that others need to imitate. Do you see that creativity applies to all aspects of the Christian life?

How tragic it is when women have great abilities that are expended in ways that will not last. Sadly, there are women calling themselves disciples whose creative strengths are not focused on the kingdom of God, but on selfish pursuits. This is nothing less than a prostitution of their energies—giving away their best and most sacred for the world, for that which is only temporary:

- Women who are great at "networking" at the office, but can't seem to figure out how to pull together with women from church...
- Women who are ambitious to make sales for the company, but are resistant to offer their greatest commodity, Jesus Christ...
- Women who have been trained to educate in the secular world, but are too tired to teach children at church...
- Women who have acquired administrative and organizational abilities, but are too busy to organize a fellowship meal...

God gave us all of our gifts; we must use them to bring him honor.

Order and a Plan

The creation is just one example of the orderliness of God. Throughout Scripture I have found that God has a place for all things...and he knows where it is! Noah's ark (which will be discussed later) had to be of exact measurements. The same held true for the tabernacle and the ark of the covenant. The temple, the clothes of the priests, the sacrifices—God made it clear how he wanted each to be. With the birth of the church, God planned that each person in the body should have a use, a function in building up the church. Nothing and no one is wasted. God's plan is always clear.

Our world today is very helpful in providing all kinds of "time-saving" guides that we can use to help us order our lives. Appointment calendars of all types, shapes and styles abound in the marketplace. But too often, women live their days "flying by the seat of their pants"—without goals, without plans, without dreams. Do you find yourself disorganized, spacy, forgetting things? Are you frequently late? Do you arrive for appointments rushed, stressed and discombobulated? Do you lie in bed at night wondering if you have accomplished anything productive that day? This is not how God wants you to live! "Well, I'm just a spontaneous person!" you say. That's great, but do your friends and family suffer because you don't live up to your word? Spontaneity and flexibility are admirable traits that should be used to benefit others, not just "because I felt like it." Without structure in our lives, spontaneity loses its meaning. In fact, it is more correctly labeled "irresponsibility."

"Girls Just Wanna Have Fun." This song title describes many women, and certainly there's nothing wrong with having fun—I kind of like it myself. But if that is all my life is about, I'm in big trouble. I'm so grateful to have a cause to believe in, a purpose for my life: to bring glory to God and to help others to do the same. If we do not have a definite order and plan to our daily lives, however, we can easily lose sight of our purpose and become distracted.

Fun, career, family—these are all important aspects of life that demand our time and energy. But what's the point? What's the purpose of it all? If each endeavor is an end in itself, it leads to frustration and a lack of fulfillment. Disciples must remember their purpose in everything they do. Just as God had a plan and a purpose for creation, I have to have a plan for my own life...for my days. Every day I must keep my mission in the forefront of my mind, and make decisions regarding my usage of time from the perspective of that mission.

Before I was married one of my jobs happened to be at a printing company. I had this job because I had to make a living and pay the bills. But I was convinced I also had this job so that I could share my faith with those who worked around me. "Sharing my faith" didn't necessarily involve inviting someone to church; it involved thinking of ways to somehow let my conversation be "seasoned with salt," as the Bible instructs us in Colossians 4:6. I knew I was making an impact when one of the graphic artists who worked with me, in the course of a conversation, declared: "Kay, you'd bring up God if we were talking about toilet paper!" Now, I knew her complaint was a bit exaggerated, (What did God have to do with toilet paper?) but inwardly I was pleased that she saw God as so important to me. Although she never responded to the gospel, one of the salesmen we did business with did, and I felt like my time there served its purpose!

Confidence

God looked at each aspect of creation and proclaimed: "It is good." When he finished his work on the sixth day, he went even further: "It is very good." God was very pleased with what he had done. He was confident that what he had done was good.

Confidence is the quality that is often the "missing link" in so many women's characters. Insecurity and low self-esteem are weights that drag us down from the height to which God has called us. Thousands of books, magazine articles, television shows, doctors and therapists have tried to solve the problem. Most will agree that confidence comes when we can be pleased with our lives, when we can look at our accomplishments and feel good about them.

Most of us have asked these age-old questions at some point in our lives: "What am I doing here? What's my life all about?" Those questions were all too familiar to me before I knew God. Memories of lying in bed at night, with the busyness of the day behind me, questioning my existence are still clear in my mind.

But for me, another memory stands out even clearer. I had been a Christian for just a few months, and was still in college. I had started off that day praying and reading the Bible. Later, I had spent great time sharing my life with Chris-

tian friends, and had invited other friends to join me in studying the Bible and attending church. Determined to give my
very best in my studies at school, I was working hard. I was at
a point where I had dealt radically with the "outward sins" in
my life and was tenaciously tackling the "inward" ones. As I
was walking through the hall of my sorority house that day, I
recall being hit with the realization: "I am living the way God
wants me to live!" The peace, the confidence and the joy that
I felt were so new and real to me that the wonder of that
moment and that thought stays with me to this day.

I admit that my confidence level has wavered through the
years. I've had times of incredible insecurity, being prey to
consuming questions like: "What do others think? What will
others say? What do I want to do with my life?" These unset-
tling thoughts have been incredibly dangerous to me, leading
me into a downward spiral of confusion and even despair.
Like many women, I have even feigned confidence and
strength, while inside feeling as though my spine were made
of Jell-O.

True confidence comes only from being able to say in
your heart: "This is how God wants me to live!" When we
know that we are following Jesus and striving to be like him
every day, we can be pleased with our lives. It has nothing to
do with being prettier or better than someone else; it even has
nothing to do with sinlessness. Confidence has everything to
do with waking up every morning and saying: "Jesus is the
Lord of my life" and really meaning it. True confidence comes
when our cause, our creativity, and our very worth are caught
up in doing the will of God. If we don't have the aim of serving God with our lives, and if we are not efficiently and creatively fulfilling that cause, then we will never have the confidence to stand back and look at our lives and say, "It is good.
It is very good."

Creating Man and Woman

*Then God said, "Let us make man in our
image, in our likeness, and let them rule over the
fish of the sea and the birds of the air, over the live-
stock, over all the earth, and over all the creatures
that move along the ground."*

*So God created man in his own image,
    in the image of God he created him;
    male and female he created them*
(Genesis 1:26-27).

The LORD *God said, "It is not good for the man to be
alone. I will make a helper suitable for him."
...So the* LORD *God caused the man to fall into a
deep sleep; and while he was sleeping, he took one of the
man's ribs and closed up the place with flesh. Then the*
LORD *God made a woman from the rib he had taken out
of the man, and he brought her to the man.
    The man said,*

*"This is now bone of my bones
    and flesh of my flesh;
she shall be called 'woman,'
    for she was taken out of man."*

*...The man and his wife were both naked, and they
felt no shame (Genesis 2:18, 21-25).*

The scriptural announcement of the beginning of mankind proclaims this: "God has had children! Twins! He's
named them *man* and *woman*." God's proclamation defies all
racism, sexism, nationalism and hatred. Humanity has been
created in his image, and we are all his sons and daughters.

What a different world this would be if we could all recognize the image of God in our fellowman.

The verses that describe the creation of man and woman emphasize what God is trying to impress upon us throughout Scripture: Human beings are special, unique and dearly cared for. After forming his first son and daughter, he gave them a job to do (1:28), provided food for them, and placed them in an atmosphere of beauty.

The Home

The location of the Garden of Eden is uncertain, although it has been placed in what was known as Southeast Mesopotamia (modern-day Iraq). What is sure, however, is the loveliness of this place. It was filled with all kinds of trees that were pleasing to the eye and good for food. The garden was watered by a main river that separated into four rivers, one of which led to the land of Havilah, a place of incredible richness and beauty (possibly Armenia). The garden and all that lived there were under the rule of the man and the woman. Most beautiful of all was that God himself made a habit of walking freely there and enjoying communion with them. It was, indeed, a paradise.

I always like to look at the Garden of Eden and compare it to a modern-day home. The ideal home is one where all members work together, where food is provided in a pleasant atmosphere, and where God is obviously present—in the lives of the family. Home is a place of beauty, order and purpose, all wrapped up in the presence of love. God must have known that people need to encounter beauty in their everyday lives.

Several years ago while we were working with the church in Tokyo, Japan, I understood more clearly this need to see beauty. My husband and I, our two children and a nanny were sharing a cramped little two-room apartment overlooking a crowded street on one side and a drainage canal on the other. Tokyo is so packed with people that all the living accommodations are quite small; space throughout the city is at a premium. Nevertheless, the Japanese people are masters at fashioning exquisite homes with a limited amount of room. The flower arrangements, the furnishings and the paintings all reflect an appreciation for beauty that those in wide-open spaces often take for granted. The Japanese taught me what has been true since the Garden of Eden: Our eyes need to see beauty. Beauty and order bring about a tranquillity and peace that make life so much more pleasant.

The Helper

In the Garden of Eden God gave the man a job: to work and take care of the garden (Genesis 2:15). The man needed a helper in order to do it. Note those two key words: "need" and "help." They are words that many are loathe to use today, and relationships suffer because of it. The success of relationships today, and the success of the relationship between the first man and woman, are dependent on recognizing that we need one another, and that we must help one another.

It is a humbling thing to admit that we really need another person in our lives. Adam, the first man, the perfect man, the man formed with the very hands of God, was told that it was not good for him to be alone, and that he needed a helper. He wasn't a "macho" guy who boasted, "I don't need anybody!" but rather, he submitted himself to the working of God to create just what he needed: a woman.

Before we call our husbands into the room and read aloud to them the preceding paragraph and remind them ever so sweetly of how much they need us, let us proceed to the creation of Eve. The first woman was created with one thing in mind: to help Adam. Does this bother you? Are you annoyed by the fact that woman was created to help man? Yes, this runs counter to the independent, self-sufficient woman we hear that we are supposed to be. Yes, this may make some modern feminists' hair stand on end. But, like it or not, "helping" is what we were made for.

Whatever we do in life, we must see ourselves as women whose job it is to help. Is your role in the church one of helping and serving others in any way, great or small? Do you look at your career in this way—as a service you can give to help others? How about as a wife: Are you a help to your husband, or a hindrance? Are you "suitable" for him? That is, do you study his needs and consider how to meet them?

I'm fortunate that I've been able to know many young women when they were falling in love and planning for marriage. Occasionally I've heard the comment: "I really believe *he* is the right one for me." This comment always sends up warning flags in my mind, and I've had to remind women, "Yes, but what's more important is: Are you the right one for him?" I'm convinced that a woman must enter the marriage relationship with a heart to give and to help her husband to be the best he can be. I also trust in God's promises that when we do it God's way, he will allow our best abilities and talents to be used. God will make sure we reach our full potential.

When the first woman was formed, she was not considered inferior or less important, but equally significant in God's plans. Paul reminds us that though woman was created for man, men and women are interdependent:

> *In the Lord, however, woman is not independent of man, nor is man independent of woman. For as woman came from man, so also man is born of woman. But everything comes from God (1 Corinthians 11:11-12).*

Scriptures confirm that God loves women and is the greatest advocate for their happiness, well-being, safety and fulfillment. If you believe this, then you'll be happy to be a "helper." If you don't, you need to study, pray, get advice and change your mind and heart to be obedient to God's plan. You will not be peaceful or content until you do!

Resting from His Work

By the seventh day God had finished the work he had been doing; so on the seventh day he rested from all his work. And God blessed the seventh day and made it holy, because on it he rested from all the work of creating that he had done (Genesis 2:2-3).

The creation complete, God chose the seventh day to rest from the work he had accomplished. This by no means implies that God's energy was depleted or that the Almighty was tired, but he sets forth a pattern to be imitated throughout the centuries. Later, when the law was given to Moses, God used this example to teach the Israelites about the need for one day to rest from their labor and focus on their Creator. The Sabbath was established to remind the Jews that their work was good, but that it was God who would take care of all their needs. It should remind them that whether they worked or not, he was their ultimate provider. The Sabbath was also given to confirm the covenant that the Jews had with God: He was their God and they were his chosen people.

When Jesus walked the earth, the issue of the Sabbath became a source of tension between him and the leaders of the Jewish people. The Pharisees and teachers of the law had developed all kinds of rules about the Sabbath: how far one could walk, how much one could lift, etc. This became such a sore subject that even the compassionate acts of healing were looked upon with disdain if they were done on the Sabbath day. Jesus consistently revealed the truth and purpose of the Sabbath, although the people often responded with scorn and derision, preferring their own "wisdom" to God's.

The ultimate lesson for us as disciples is to remember what is taught in <u>Hebrews 4:9-11</u>:

> *There remains, then, a Sabbath-rest for the people of*
> *God; for anyone who enters God's rest also rests from*
> *his own work, just as God did from his. Let us, there-*
> *fore, make every effort to enter that rest....*

Just as the Israelites were to confirm the covenant by remembering the Sabbath, Christians must daily confirm their covenant with Christ. As the Israelites were to remember the source of their help, Christians are to remember that Jesus is the source of their salvation. The Israelites were to trust in God to provide, and Christians are to trust completely in the help of Jesus.

On a very practical, everyday level we can learn from the Sabbath that it is okay for us to rest too. When we plan well and use our time well, we can also fit into our schedules a time to relax, to rest, to re-create without feeling guilty about all we need to be doing. When we run ourselves into the ground because of guilt and disorganization, we are not imitating the example of our creator God.

Our family leads such a busy life that we look forward to the few days we can go on a short trip to "re-create" ourselves and draw closer to one another. These vacations usually consist of going to the beach, playing cards and just "hanging out." Having this time of relaxation helps us to come back home with the energy and enthusiasm we need in order to be effective and productive. We have also strengthened our relationships and have made memories that will last a lifetime.

In the beginning, God. In the end, God. At all times, God. Creation sets all things in order, and reminds us that God is at the center of it all: directing, planning and providing a life for mankind. As we continue to study the history of *Our Beginning*, we would do well to keep in mind what the Psalmist said many centuries later, reminding us to praise the creator God:

> *Praise the* LORD.
>
> *Praise the* LORD *from the heavens,*
>   *praise him in the heights above.*
> *Praise him, all his angels,*
>   *praise him, all his heavenly hosts.*
> *Praise him, sun and moon,*
>   *praise him, all you shining stars.*
> *Praise him, you highest heavens*
>   *and you waters above the skies.*
> *Let them praise the name of the* LORD,
>   *for he commanded and they were created.*
> *He set them in place for ever and ever;*
>   *he gave a decree that will never pass away.*
>
> *Praise the* LORD *from the earth,*
>   *you great sea creatures and all ocean depths,*
> *lightning and hail, snow and clouds,*
>   *stormy winds that do his bidding,*
> *you mountains and all hills,*
>   *fruit trees and all cedars,*
> *wild animals and all cattle,*
>   *small creatures and flying birds,*
> *kings of the earth and all nations,*
>   *you princes and all rulers on earth,*
> *young men and maidens,*
>   *old men and children.*

Let them praise the name of the LORD,
  for his name alone is exalted;
  his splendor is above the earth and the heavens.
He has raised up for his people a horn,
  the praise of all his saints,
  of Israel, the people close to his heart.

Praise the LORD.

Psalm 148

· *Taking It Home* ·

1. What does it mean to you to know that God had a plan to bless your life before the creation of the world?

2. How has the light of God's presence made a difference in your life? What corners of darkness have been exposed to God's healing light?

3. In what ways do you think God wants you to be creative? What do you need to do to use your creative abilities more extensively to build up the kingdom?

4. Do you "fly by the seat of your pants" daily, or do you have goals, plans and dreams? Are you true to your word in both big and little ways?

5. Are you able to look at your life and say, "I am living the way God wants me to live"? In what area do you need and want to change in order to be able to say this (remembering that we are not talking about perfection)?

6. Think about your home, whether it is a room in your family's house, a dorm room, an apartment (flat) or a house. Do you seek to reflect God's creation, to

make it a place of beauty, order and purpose? In which of these three areas are you strongest? In which are you weakest? What commitment will you make to change that weakness into a strength?

7. How do you respond to the fact that God made woman to be a helper to man? No matter your role in life, married or single, do you enjoy being a helper to others? If you are married, how can you best help your husband? Do you pray to be a suitable helper every day?

8. Do you feel guilty when you slow down for a few minutes of rest or relaxation? Or do you stay slowed down too long? How does understanding God's rest on the seventh day help you to gear your schedule to include valid periods of rest and reflection?

The
Woe

3

Genesis
3

The man and his wife were both naked,
and they felt no shame.

GENESIS 2:25

A Day in the Garden

Have you seen those advertisements on television or in magazines promoting a vacation in the Caribbean, or in Hawaii, or some other tropical isle? There is usually a photograph of a couple walking down a sandy beach hand in hand, the turquoise sea shimmering like diamonds with a vibrant sunset in the background. "Oh, to be in a place like that," you might say. "It would be paradise!"

Well, that's *my* idea of a great vacation. What's yours? Is it also an exotic island? Or is it a mountaintop cabin, or a camping spot in the cool of the woods? Whatever your idea of paradise might be, it can't even come close to what Adam and Eve enjoyed in the Garden of Eden.

Paradise

"Paradise" is defined as a place or a state of bliss. Indeed, this is what the first man and woman had in the garden, their home. They had all the comforts they could want. They had a beautiful place in which to live, plenty of delicious food to eat, clear sparkling water to drink. They had each other. They had God as their companion and friend.

It was this close, personal relationship with God that made the garden a true paradise. No matter how luxurious our surroundings, they will leave us empty if God is not present. Adam and Eve lived in a state of perfection: unity with God and unity in their relationship with one another. No scars or hurts or pains from the past, no guilt or regret—only the love for God and the love for one another in their hearts.

This description of paradise should remind us of our final destination: heaven. Throughout Scripture, heaven is described with festive or elaborate imagery: weddings, banquets, streets of gold, and so on—images that represent what we think of as good or pleasurable. The most wonderful thing about heaven, though, is that we will be with God. The book of Revelation tells us that there will be no crying, no pain, no mourning, no death, and that God himself will be with us and will personally wipe every tear from our eyes. This will be our paradise: experiencing time without end, being filled with love for one another, being at total peace in our hearts, and loving, adoring, praising and worshipping God.

In a very real way, when we're ushered into heaven, it will be like going back to the Garden of Eden—a perfect existence with a perfect God. Adam and Eve let go of it, but because of Jesus we can take hold of it.

Paradise Lost

In fairy tales, movies and romantic love stories, the hero and heroine ride off into the sunset and "live happily ever after." This is not the case with Adam and Eve. What starts as a beautiful adventure in paradise becomes a nightmare, a tale of darkness and woe. How did it all go wrong?

> *Now the serpent was more crafty than any of the*
> *wild animals the* LORD *God had made. He said to the*
> *woman, "Did God really say, 'You must not eat from*
> *any tree in the garden'?"*
>
> *The woman said to the serpent, "We may eat fruit*
> *from the trees in the garden, but God did say, 'You*
> *must not eat fruit from the tree that is in the middle of*
> *the garden, and you must not touch it, or you will die.'"*
>
> *"You will not surely die," the serpent said to the*
> *woman (Genesis 3:1-4).*

Thus far in the history of humankind, we have been introduced to God, Adam and Eve, and the animals. We have witnessed the beginning of humanity, the birth of God's relationship with his creation. But here, early in our history, we see the beginning of the end. At this point a character enters who is the epitome of craftiness, guile and deceit. This is Satan, and he marks his entrance with an insidious lie.

Deceit, falsehood, lying, fraudulence: These bring about the woe of mankind. The serpent starts his cunning argument by stating a half-truth to Eve. She and Adam *were* permitted to eat the fruit of any tree, save one. Eve immediately corrects his statement, and Satan then places a doubt her mind. He causes her to begin to distrust God, to impugn his motives, and to suppose that she knows what is best for her happiness and well-being. The temptation of Eve is accomplished not simply by compelling her to eat the fruit, but by tricking her into believing a lie.

The Deceiver

What worked with Eve can work with anyone. Why should Satan change his tactics today? As you read through the book of Genesis, you will notice many instances in which problems and heartaches are caused by deceit. As you read the Gospels, you will see that Satan even tempted Jesus using Scripture fallaciously. Later, he used rumors and half-truths in trying to stop the growth of the early church.

But Jesus "had Satan's number." He called him the "father of lies" and said that lying was his native language (John 8:44). Today, Satan's nature and tactics haven't changed. Satan knows the havoc he can wreak on any woman at any time by causing her to believe a lie. Any disciple worth her salt must be aware of how Satan works, and must realize how easily she can begin to believe his lies if she is not careful.

There are no "white lies" or "black lies," no "little lies" or "big lies," there are only lies. Satan, however, does use different types of lies. If we are aware of his tactics, we will then be able to catch him in his lies. As we look at the woe that came into the world through the sins of Adam and Eve, and later, the sins of their son Cain, we can see different motivations and several types of lies. We will examine three types of lies: the world's lies, religious lies and lies of self-preservation. As we are able to recognize these lies, we can begin to break the web of deceit in ourselves and in the lives of those we love.

Lies of Satan

The World's Lies

> *Do not love the world or anything in the world. If anyone loves the world, the love of the Father is not in him. For everything in the world—the cravings of sinful man, the lust of his eyes and the boasting of what he has and does—comes not from the Father but from the world (1 John 2:15-16).*

When Satan used this "worldly" type of lie, he convinced Eve how good the forbidden fruit would be to eat. She was persuaded that the fruit was good for food and pleasing to the eye and was desirable for gaining wisdom. All in all, she believed the lie that living without obedience to God was OK. "I don't have to do what God says," she might have thought. "I can do what *I* think is best."

I suppose the biggest lie that the world wants us to believe has to do with what is really important in life. Turn on the TV, open the newspaper, flip through a magazine...at school, at work and at play, we are all programmed to believe that God is unnecessary in our lives. The lie may be through a blatant endorsement of atheism, or it may be of a more insidious nature: It's fine to have God in your life "somewhere," but certainly not as master or *Lord*. Oh, sure. Go to church, give God some superficial thanks at special holidays or when you have accomplished some worthwhile goals, but don't let it go any further than that! What's *really* important is to make money, to be successful, to get an education, to be popular, beautiful or talented.

Frankly, I am fed up with artists and athletes who give lip service to "the good Lord above" for all their accomplishments, and then continue in a lifestyle of decadence. As disciples, we can't be sucked into a way of thinking that compromises the expectations of God. The world wants us to believe that we can live however we want; that we can go after our desires without considering whether they are pleasing to God. The lie packs its punch by convincing us that living for this world is going to fulfill us: "It doesn't get any better than this." Right?

I distinctly recall placing an entry in my diary about a year before I became a Christian. "I want to be worldly," I wrote. At the time of that writing, I had no comprehension of what it meant from a biblical viewpoint. It simply had to do with the goals in my life. I wanted to learn about everything—to experience life fully. I wanted to travel, to experiment with drugs and sex, to become educated and to understand religion. (I am glad I had the latter desire. Although I only wanted a taste of religious faith, God used that to lead me to him.)

I, like millions of others, had been duped by the lie that the world would provide my fulfillment, and that even if I did "find" God, he would only be a diminutive aspect of my full "worldly" life. We can see the tragic results this lie brings about. Beginning with Eve, women continue to be conned into a meaningless life, pursuing some elusive promised happiness that doesn't exist. This is the lie that was born into our world and grows daily like a consuming cancer.

Even after we become Christians we can find ourselves bombarded with these deceitful attacks from Satan. On the "top ten" list of Satan's inventions, we can recognize some subtle and not so subtle fabrications he wants us to fall for:

1. You can never change. Your upbringing and the choices you have made in the past make you what you are, and it is futile to try to be anything different.
2. Don't trust anyone; people will only disappoint you.
3. You can be religious, but don't be a fanatic. You don't want to turn people off.
4. It's fine to miss church every once in a while if something important comes up.
5. Don't ever let anyone ever tell you what to do. They don't understand your special situation.
6. Once you've been sexually promiscuous, you won't ever be able to have a really pure lifestyle. It's embedded in your brain and body and you can't give it up.
7. You can't say who is a Christian and who is not. After all, the Bible says, "Don't judge."
8. It's just too hard to live as a disciple.

9. There is no one in my town/school/workplace who is open to learning about God.
10. If I leave the church, I can always come back later.

Satan mixes a little bit of truth in his falsehoods; that is exactly why he is so successful. He is tricky; otherwise we would not be so easily misled. We must be able to discern what is good and throw out the rest!

Religious Lies

The Spirit clearly says that in later times some will abandon the faith and follow deceiving spirits and things taught by demons. Such teachings come through hypocritical liars, whose consciences have been seared as with a hot iron (1 Timothy 4:1-2).

For the time will come when men will not put up with sound doctrine. Instead, to suit their own desires, they will gather around them a great number of teachers to say what their itching ears want to hear. They will turn their ears away from the truth and turn aside to myths (2 Timothy 4:3-4).

Satan has a tremendous knack for taking the words of God and twisting them to suit his own devices. When he told Eve that she would not die and that her understanding would increase (3:4-5), he was manipulating the truth to get Eve to do what he wanted. Certainly she would not drop dead at the first bite, but Satan knew that bite would bring about her physical death eventually, and her spiritual death immediately. His lie seemed to make sense; it was logical to a mind willing to be swayed.

The devastation that has been brought about by the use of religious lies can't even be imagined. Seekers of truth have been incredibly thwarted in their attempt to know God by those who have taken the truth of God and turned it into what was never meant to be. God's word has been taken out of context, misunderstood and abused to proliferate selfish and worldly ambitions. Looking at history shows how scriptures have been misused to an evil end: religious wars, the Inquisition, the plundering of lands, anti-Semitism, racism and oppression. These are only a few obvious examples of the tragedies caused by a distortion of God's word.

What is often not as obvious are the ways that religious lies are used in our present day to hinder true Christianity. False doctrines abound. People don't know what to believe. One church teaches one thing; another teaches the opposite. The priest says this; the preacher says that. Who's telling the truth? What should we believe? How can we know?

Of course, God does not leave us to participate in a guessing game, but provides a simple way to find out the truth. The problem is that most people find it easier to let family or friends or religious leaders spoon-feed them religious dogma rather than to take the effort and energy to search out truth for themselves. Inevitably, this allows false beliefs about what the Scriptures really teach to pervade the religious world.

The story you are about to read is true. The names have been changed to protect the guilty. Once there was a young girl named Sue. The time had come in her life when she was able to take that test that young people long to take: the test for a driving permit. This is a written, multiple-choice test, taken in order to ascertain the testee's understanding of the traffic laws of the land. Sue dutifully obtained her copy of the driver's manual, the booklet designed to teach these traffic laws. She placed the manual on her bedside table and looked at it every day. At school, Sue asked her friends about the test.

"Oh, it's easy," said Mary. "You don't need to study for it!"

"It's just common sense," said Sally. "Nobody studies for that test!"

Numerous other friends provided similar advice: "Just go on in there, smile and come out with your permit!"

So Sue took their advice, and on the day of the test she left, ready and eager to become a part of the driving public. Confidently she faced the computer terminal and began to punch in the answers. *Uh-oh, got that one wrong...oh, well, you're allowed to miss a few anyway. Oops, there's another!* To make an unpleasant story shorter, Sue left the Registry of Motor Vehicles in tears. She'd been given some questions she just didn't know the answers to, and had failed the test.

Fortunately for "Sue," it was only a driving test and could be taken again. After learning her lesson, she diligently studied the driver's manual, determined not to listen to her friends' "advice" again. She took the test, and walked out happily, permit in hand.

Hopefully, the analogy in the story is obvious to you. How many people make a similar mistake for an even greater, more significant "test"—the test of our relationship with God? It is easy to be fooled by religious lies; we must study the Scriptures for ourselves and have convictions based on truth, not on hearsay or tradition. And we need to realize that ultimately we are responsible for our own ignorance...we can blame no one else.

Lies of Self-Preservation

> *Now Cain said to his brother Abel, "Let's go out to the field." And while they were in the field, Cain attacked his brother Abel and killed him.*
>
> *Then the Lord said to Cain, "Where is your brother Abel?"*
>
> *I don't know," he replied, "Am I my brother's keeper?" (Genesis 4:8-9).*

Cain, the firstborn of Eve, had killed his own little brother. He had been jealous of Abel's success and favor with God. Even though he was specifically warned by God about the wicked attitude of his heart (4:7), Cain gave in to his hatred and murdered the source of his envy. Cain's cunning was so effective that Abel exhibited no hesitation to go out to the field with him. When called to account by God, Cain's response was one that is typical of all mankind: deceitful, defensive and elusive. First he lied about his knowledge of his brother's whereabouts, and then, in true human fashion, he tried to blame-shift. "Am I my brother's keeper?" is just another way of saying, "How could you ask me that? Back off!"

The root of so many lies is "What will make *me* look better?" This is how gossip begins and how rumors spread. We say something that makes another person look a little bit bad, which makes us look a little bit better. It is a protective device to get us out of trouble. It is leaving a false impression. It is saying something that is only half true. It is purposefully not giving the whole truth. It is not caring or trusting enough to make what we say absolutely clear.

Here are some samples of lies of self-preservation:

Innocent question: "Say, remember those neighbors you wanted to bring to church...did you go by and invite them yet?"

Not-so-innocent answer: "Oh, I went by, but they were never home!"

Truth: You drove by and the car wasn't in the driveway.

Innocent question: "Why didn't you return my call?"

Not-so-innocent answer: "I tried but your line was always busy!"

Truth: You never really tried to call.

Innocent question: "How come you were so late for work today?"
Not-so-innocent answer: "The traffic was just awful."
Truth: You also left twenty minutes late.

These answers are "not so innocent" because they sound reasonable, but are used to cover up the truth. In the quest to protect ourselves, we can find ways to be accepted and look good, or we can decide to be completely honest and take the hit if we have made a mistake.

All lies are damaging to human relationships. When we lie, we are saying we don't care enough to be open and honest with another person, that we do not respect them, that we are afraid of being hurt. This fear of being wounded does not excuse deceitfulness. Think about the lies you've been told. Whatever the reason, when you have been lied to, don't you feel betrayed? Think also about the lies you have told. Did they promote honest, truthful, deep, bonding communication? Are you closer to the person you lied to, or to the person you lied about? I think all of us would have to say No.

Sin Brings Separation

Back to that very first lie in the Garden of Eden: We can now understand where it all went wrong. After Adam and Eve partook of the forbidden fruit, they started to experience things they didn't want to experience. They knew guilt and shame for the first time. They became fearful of God, instead of welcoming his company. They hid from him. This is what sin does: It separates us from one another, and it separates us from God.

Think about what Adam and Eve might have felt when God made the garments out of animal skins. They must have been horrified to have to cover themselves with the skins of the creatures who had shared the garden with them. It is important to note, however, that even after the great downfall of the first man and woman, God still cared for them. He made them clothes to cover their shame. This is a foreshadowing of the way God covers our shame even today. It took the death of his Son, Jesus, to cover our sins. Christ gave his life, and now we are clothed in him: "...for all of you who were baptized into Christ have clothed yourselves with Christ" (Galatians 3:27).

Lies brought about Adam and Eve's exclusion from the garden, their spiritual death, and the alienation of their oldest son. Lies are horrendous. We must vow to ourselves and to those we love that deceit will not be on our lips or in our hearts. And we have a great example to follow in Jesus. Look at the following scriptures that show the honesty and integrity of our Lord:

> *He committed no sin, and no deceit was found in his mouth (1 Peter 2:22).*
>
> *...it is impossible for God to lie... (Hebrews 6:18).*
>
> *...God, who does not lie... (Titus 1:2).*
>
> *...grace and truth came through Jesus Christ (John 1:17).*

When Jesus first met Nathanael, he said of him, "Here is a true Israelite, in whom there is nothing false" (John 1:47). What a refreshing and encouraging description of a person. I'd love to be described similarly: "She doesn't have a deceitful bone in her body." When I consider how deceitfulness has destroyed so much, it places a yearning in my heart for complete honesty and integrity and truthfulness. I want to help put a stop to the woe caused by Satan. Don't you?

· *Taking It Home* ·

1. What is your idea of a dream vacation? Describe why it would be "paradise" to you. How does this help you to get a clue about what heaven will be like?

2. Adam and Eve had everything they needed, but they were not content. How about you? Do you tend to be grateful for the blessings God has given you, or do you tend to be dissatisfied and want more?

3. Does heaven seem real to you? Can you imagine an existence where there is no crying, no pain, no mourning, no death? Can you imagine actually being in the presence of God himself? When you stop and remind yourself that heaven *is* real, how does it affect the way you view this life?

4. Satan is indeed the "father of lies." Are you daily aware of the lies he tells you? List some of them. How can you know for sure that these are lies? How have you learned to combat them so they will not cause "woe" in your life?

5. Has Satan ever fooled you into believing that what is really important is to make money, to be successful, to get an education, to be popular or to be talented? What was the result when you went after any of these things in order to find your happiness?

6. Do you believe that the following is a true statement: Religious lies are the most deceptive of them all? Why? How have you been deceived by religious lies? How did God work to open your eyes?

7. Do you have deep convictions about telling "white lies"? About slanting or shading the truth to make yourself look better? Why is it so important to have deep convictions in this area? When you are not being careful and responsible with what you say, how does it affect your relationships?

8. Jesus said Nathanael was a person "in whom there is nothing false." Isn't that a refreshing comment to hear...especially about yourself? Is there anything false that you are aware of that you want to get rid of?

The
Witnesses

4

Genesis
5–9

*When God created man, he made him in the like-
ness of God. He created them male and female and
blessed them. And when they were created, he called
them "man."*

*When Adam had lived 130 years, he had a son in
his own likeness, in his own image; and he named
him Seth. After Seth was born, Adam lived 800 years
and had other sons and daughters. Altogether, Adam
lived 930 years, and then he died.*

GENESIS 5:1B-5

It is God's desire to help us understand not only our be-
ginnings, but our purpose as well—to be in relationship with a
loving, faithful God. In a courtroom, no case can be won, no
point can be proven without the presence of reliable witnesses.
To make his point with clarity and power, God "calls to the
stand" reliable witnesses to speak to mankind generation after generation. His witness might be as intangible as the death
experience, as physical as a pile of stones, or as human and
vulnerable as the men and women of the Bible. Some of these
witnesses are introduced to us in Genesis, chapters five through
nine: death (the cycle of life), Enoch and Noah.

Death

Yearning for Family

Family planning is not a twentieth-century phenomenon. It had its origins with God. He desired to have children and to bless them. He yearned for a family; he craved the companionship of human beings and planned to shower upon them the blessings of this earth, which was created for their satisfaction. If you are like most women, you can relate to that yearning God had for children. Some of my very first memories of childhood involve playing with dolls and pretending to be a mommy. I loved and cared for "Lu-Lu," one of my first dolls, who, in fact, is still around—shabby and old, but a reminder of my vision for the future. As I grew up, that desire never waned: One of my greatest goals in life was to have children to love and to nurture. I hoped that they would resemble me and love me, and that we, together with their dad, would form a happy family.

The desire to give life is one of the things we have in common with God. He planned and created men and women who would carry in their likeness a resemblance to him. That resemblance was darkened in the Garden when Adam and Eve sinned. Their disobedience brought about a spiritual death and, ultimately, a physical death. Even though it took hundreds of years, Adam's life did come to an end.

The Cycle of Life

The fifth chapter of Genesis has a recurring theme: People keep being born and people keep dying. In fact, in just that short chapter, the phrase, "and he died," is repeated eight times. The chapter records the cycle of life: birth, reproduction and finally, death.

Death is not exactly the most pleasant topic, is it? We don't like to think about it because we don't want it to happen.

When we try to give instructions to our loved ones in case of death (the need for a will, funeral arrangements, life insurance, etc.), the result is usually awkwardness, hesitation and resistance. We want to pretend that we will live forever and that death is something we won't have to face.

Yet death is a fact of life. It strikes all ages, races, genders, cultures. I saw death suddenly take my father at the age of fifty-five due to a massive heart attack. I mourned when death struck a school friend who was robbed, beaten and thrown into a canal to drown. I watched as death attacked a young mother who lost her battle with Hodgkin's Disease. I've lost grandparents in their old age and college friends in their youth. I've lost friends to accidents, illnesses and most horribly, to suicide.

Death is indeed sad; it is something we often dread and fear. Wouldn't it be nice to have someone else go through it first, and be able to come back and tell us what it's like? As a child, I often would ask my older brother about the things I looked forward to—either with fear or with excitement. He was the first one to go off to kindergarten, to spend the night away from home, to go to junior high school, to drive a car, to go to college. All his experiences were proof to me that I could do the same things with success. As disciples, Jesus is our "older brother" who has gone through the experience of death, and was raised from the dead to reassure us that there is more, that there is life after death. Hebrews 2:14-15 states,

> *...he too shared in their humanity so that by his death*
> *he might destroy him who holds the power of death—*
> *that is, the devil—and free those who all their lives*
> *were held in slavery by their fear of death.*

The imminence of death can be a positive thing. I recently witnessed the baptism of a woman in Paris who had been powerfully influenced by the thought of death—her own. This woman's husband had been unfaithful to her in the past, and unfortunately became infected with HIV. Knowing that he carried this deadly disease, he had sexual relations with his wife without informing her of the danger. Later, when she contracted AIDS, the truth came out. Everyone in the family was infuriated at the father and wanted nothing to do with him for what he had done to his wife.

Everyone, that is, except one of his daughters, who happens to be a disciple. She had compassion on her father, and against the objections of the rest of the family continued to love him and reach out to him. Her devotion to him touched his heart and made him open to the gospel. When he became ill, he was all the more eager to get his life right with God and to ask for forgiveness from his wife. He was baptized shortly before his death.

His wife noticed all the changes in her husband, and saw the unconditional love of her daughter. She too was touched, and wanted to learn about Jesus. When it became obvious to the doctors that her death was drawing near, she asked to leave the hospital one more time—to get baptized. I watched her daughter immerse her in the waters of baptism, and then as she left to return to the hospital, I realized with a lump in my throat that I might never see this woman again until we all are in heaven together. Praise God that when she does die, she will die reconciled with him.

Our Lives Must Count

A friend of mine was recently preparing dinner for her family with the help of her young daughter. The child was excited and happy that a friend of the family, a teenage girl, had made the decision to be baptized. As they worked together, the daughter chattered on about the natural course of life. "First, you get baptized and become a Christian, and that's awesome! Then you get married; then you have children, and then, you get to die, and that's awesome too 'cause you get to go to heaven!" This little girl understands life better than most adults!

Each one of us is a participant in the cycle of life, just like Adam and Seth and Enosh and Kenan and Mahalalel, and so on. Our lives today will not last for the same number of years as those in the fifth chapter of Genesis: Whether due to the protected environment of this time period, or the genetic purity of the individuals, or simply because of God's desire to have it be so, people lived extraordinarily long lives compared to today's average life span. In contrast, we now have the debilitating effects of disease, pollution and bad genes that cause our lives to be much shorter than the average of 700 years. However long or short our days may be, death can be a reminder, a witness, that life is to be lived and that our days must count for something.

Enoch

> *When Enoch had lived 65 years, he became the father of Methuselah. And after he became the father of Methuselah, Enoch walked with God 300 years and had other sons and daughters. Altogether, Enoch lived 365 years. Enoch walked with God; then he was no more, because God took him away (Genesis 5:21-24).*

Lifelong Devotion

In the genealogical listing of the descendants of Adam, there is one divergence from the standard course of birth, life and death. Enoch is an example of one whose dedication to God did not wane through the years. He had a relationship with God so deep that God simply took him away from this

earth. He took a shortcut to heaven, bypassing death altogether. The only other occurrence of this kind is when Elijah
was taken into heaven (2 Kings 2:11). (And lest you think it
was easier "back then" to live a life devoted to God, read Jude
14-15, which reveals the ungodliness of those times.) Enoch
did not live like the rest; therefore, he did not die like the rest.

How long have *you* been walking with God? One year?
Five years? Twenty years? None of us can match the number of
years that Enoch walked with God. It is commendable to be
devoted when we are just starting our walk with God. It is also
commendable to be devoted during the positive "chapters" of
our lives—when circumstances are favorable, when the blessings of God are obviously abundant, when we are "fired up"
by great conferences and services that inspire our zeal for God.
However, nothing compares to the dedication that endures
through the rough times: the hardships and heartaches and
difficulties of life.

Run the Race

The Christian life is not like running a sprint—a fast race
started with great enthusiasm and finished in a flash. The
Christian life is more accurately likened to running a marathon, with its peaks and valleys, its bursts of fresh energy and
bouts of fatigue. The outstanding quality of a marathon run-
ner is her stubborn determination to finish that which she set
out to do. She will never quit. Her purpose is before her, and
giving up is out of the question.

The Boston Marathon is a 26-mile race that attracts thousands of runners from all over the world. It involves a gruel-
ing run from a small town outside of Boston right into the
center of the city. Rain or shine, hot or cold (it takes place in
April in New England, so one never knows!) it requires gut-
level determination to make it through "heartbreak hill" all
the way to the finish line. I'm always inspired by marathons,
but I've never been as inspired as I was after the race of 1996.

The winner in the women's division was a German by the name of Uta Pippig, who had some "little problems" as she called it, during the race. Her "little problems" were intestinal cramps that brought on diarrhea, as well as a heavy menstrual flow. Neither of these "little problems" could be hidden as she ran. Everyone thought she was too weak and too far behind to ever win the race. Most wondered if she would even be able to finish it at all. But she kept going, overtaking the lead woman from behind. In what was called "one of the most amazing finishes in marathon history," Pippig jubilantly crossed the finish line, and the roar of the crowd went up, saluting a woman who wouldn't let anything keep her from accomplishing her goal. I've never met Uta Pippig, but I will always be grateful for her example to all Christian women to keep on running the race for God.

I have been running the Christian marathon for many years now. I've had an abundance of energetic, flying, wind-in-my-hair experiences. I've also had stumbling, crawling, inching-forward-by-my-fingernails experiences. Compared to Enoch, my marathon is still in the beginning stages, and if God wills, I've got a lot of running left to do. I'm resolved to see this race to the end.

Enoch was a man who bore witness to the fact that a long, dedicated walk with God is possible. No matter how old we are, no matter what we've been through, no matter what the future holds, we must have that stubborn determination to walk with God forever. Several lines from the song "Oh Sacred Head" capture the spirit of Enoch, and this must be our prayer as well:

> Oh make me thine forever,
> and should I fainting be,
> Lord let me never, never
> outlive my love for thee.

Noah

> The LORD *saw how great man's wickedness on the earth had become, and that every inclination of the thoughts of his heart was only evil all the time. The* LORD *was grieved that he had made man on the earth, and his heart was filled with pain. So the* LORD *said, "I will wipe mankind, whom I have created, from the face of the earth—men and animals, and creatures that move along the ground, and birds of the air—for I am grieved that I have made them." But Noah found favor in the eyes of the* LORD.

> *This is the account of Noah.*

> *Noah was a righteous man, blameless among the people of his time, and he walked with God. Noah had three sons: Shem, Ham and Japheth.*

> *Now the earth was corrupt in God's sight and was full of violence. God saw how corrupt the earth had become, for all the people on earth had corrupted their ways (Genesis 6:5-12).*

The Heartbreak of God

The sad thing about living a long time is that people have more opportunities to do evil. Instead of using the time that God had given them to turn to him for blessings and love, the people of Noah's day used their time to think of all the wrong and sinful things they could do...and then they did them! This kind of lifestyle is mirrored in Romans 1:29-31:

> *They have become filled with every kind of wicked-ness, evil, greed and depravity. They are full of envy, murder, strife, deceit and malice. They are gossips, slan-*

derers, God-haters, insolent, arrogant and boastful;
they invent ways of doing evil; *they disobey their
parents; they are senseless, faithless, heartless, ruth-
less (emphasis added).*

Although varying degrees of this type of amorality and
immorality can be found in all people around the globe and
throughout history, there are times and places that seem to
epitomize ungodliness. Several years ago my husband and I
were leading a mission team to Munich, Germany. During
our time there, we visited the remains of Dachau, the model
concentration camp during the Nazi era. The camp was originally created to house political prisoners, but in the course of
time, Jews, gypsies, anti-Nazi clergymen and anyone unpopu-
lar with the regime were imprisoned there.

As I walked through this camp, I viewed barracks that
were built to accommodate 5,000 prisoners, but learned that
30,000 prisoners were barely surviving there when the libera-
tors arrived. I saw photographs of starving men staring with
hopeless eyes. I read official documents that authorized "scientific" experiments on human beings: tests to learn how much
freezing temperature the human body could withstand before
succumbing to death, experiments that measured the effects
of high altitudes on the brain, medical observations on pa-
tients who had been injected with malaria or sepsis, or who
were forced to drink sea water so that scientists could observe
the results. These types of inhumane treatment were only a
portion of the cruelty that occurred in Dachau and the other
camps. Records of beatings, torture, untreated disease, hard
labor and mass executions elicit a sense of heaviness and fore-
boding throughout the facility. I walked into the crematorium
and saw where thousands of corpses had been disposed of—
quickly, quietly and without regret.

As I wandered around on the dirt paths from building to

building, my emotions varied from fury to overwhelming sorrow. I recall standing in the area where prisoners would line up for roll call and be shot to death if they were too weak to stand. It was there that I prayed with tears, "God, how am I supposed to feel? I know that you cared for these people, so how could you allow this to happen?" I do not believe I was doubting or questioning God at that time; I simply didn't understand how to deal with all my emotions.

The answer that came to me at that moment, and that stays with me to this day, was simply, *This is how men treat one another when they forget about God.* Cruelty and inhumane treatment are the result of souls who have turned away from God and have lived according to their own selfish desires. Any people, any race, any culture, any nation that neglects their Creator is doomed. The absence of God in the hearts of men and women is to blame for horrible events such as the Holocaust.

Such was the case during the days of Noah. The earth was corrupt and full of violence, and it grieved God. He had incredible sorrow for what his people had done to themselves, and for what they had done to one another, just as a parent might grieve over a child who is turning away from all that is good and is destroying his or her life.

Was God really sorry that he had even made man on the earth? He was not regretting the act of creation, but God knew the goodness and joy that were available and that had been rejected. He understood the torture that people were bringing upon themselves, and hurt deeply for them as victims of self-induced destruction. God's understanding and knowledge about the devastation of sin was so real that his heart broke for these lost souls.

One of the greatest joys in life for a woman is to learn that she is carrying a child—that she and her husband have created a new life out of their love for one another. Years ago, the surprising news that my husband and I were expecting our first child was a delight to us and to all of our friends and family. As I pondered over the life growing inside of me, I prayed that this child would be born healthy and would grow up to love God and to serve him forever. But I also cried as I prayed that if, for some reason, this child were to someday reject God and not become a Christian, that God would take him or her before birth. Yes, I was willing to lose my baby, as devastating as that was. Pouring my heart out to him, I told God that I would rather have no children at all than to have a child who would not make it to heaven for eternity. It was (and is) my deep conviction that the only thing that counts is a right relationship with God. I prayed the same prayer while pregnant with my second child and am grateful beyond words that both of my children, in their early teen years, made the decision to be disciples. It would have broken my heart to see them rebel against God.

My sentiments are only an inkling of what God feels for all of humanity and for the people who were lost in sin during the time of Noah. Sometimes I've heard people ask, "Why doesn't God just wipe out sin?" The only way he could do that would be to wipe out all people. Sending the flood is the closest God has come to wiping out all the sinfulness of the world.

Even in the midst of that sinful world, God exhibited mercy by saving a remnant of mankind. He saw a man who was a stubborn pursuer of righteousness, a faithful man who would be the hope for the continuation of all humanity. Noah was not a perfect man, but one who was willing to be different, one who had a holy fear of God (Hebrews 11:7), and one who demonstrated a commitment to do the work God had called him to do.

To the Work

> *Noah did everything just as God commanded him (Genesis 6:22).*

Noah was asked to do something that, from his perspective, must have been completely unreasonable. Never before had there been rain comparable to the amount God was describing, and this type of natural disaster was unfathomable. The size of the ark to be built defied common sense, and the thought of gathering thousands of animals was ludicrous. But Noah was the kind of guy who was willing to be radical. He didn't care that others might laugh. He didn't mind if his new career was looked at as bizarre. Noah had a job to do, and he stuck to it until the job was done.

The labor involved in building this ark must have been incredible. Apparently, the only workers were Noah, his three sons and their wives. God was very specific about the type of wood to be used and the design and measurements of the ark. It should not amaze us too much to realize that the ratio of the width to the length of the ark is the exact ratio used by shipbuilders today. I think the size of the ark would surprise most people who have seen paintings depicting cute little boats with zebras and giraffes sticking their heads through the windows. It's like seeing postcards of the Eiffel Tower in Paris and then standing underneath it in real life. Most people's jaws drop when they see how enormous it really is. The ark, in actuality, was approximately the length of one and a half football fields, twenty-five yards wide, and as high as a four-story building. The cubic capacity has been equaled to 500 railway cars. Imagine how many animals could be carried in that much space. This was truly an awesome architectural project!

Noah was responsible for building a vessel that would provide salvation for mankind. He committed to building it before the first drop of rain fell. He obeyed God in spite of circumstances that could have caused him to doubt. He worked hard, and called his family to work hard too. What would Noah think of our commitment to the work God has called us to do?

Although God has not called anyone recently to build an ark, he has given us, as Christians, another building job to accomplish. God has called each one of us to "build up" the church—not a church building, but a body of believers who call Jesus Lord (Ephesians 4:11-13, 15-16). Our work is to lead people to the "ark" of salvation that God offers from the flood of sin that is in this world. We must be committed to building even when we can't see results, even when those around us laugh at us. We must work hard, and call our families to work hard also. Noah is our witness. He did all that God commanded. Is the same true about you?

The Covenant

> And God said, "This is the sign of the covenant I am making between me and you and every living creature with you, a covenant for all generations to come: I have set my rainbow in the clouds, and it will be the sign of the covenant between me and the earth.... Never again will the waters become a flood to destroy all life" (Genesis 9:12-13, 15b).

"It rained and poured for forty daysies, daysies. / Almost drove those animals crazy, crazy...." So goes the song that I've sung for years to my children and to children's classes as I've taught about Noah's ark and the flood. Actually, the rain itself lasted forty days, but the length of time Noah and the animals were in the ark was more like one year! (Read Genesis 7:11 through 8:14 and add it up.) It is at this point in the story that I often think about Noah's wife. I am filled with admiration for a woman who supported her husband's work, embarked upon a mission to save the world, and then spent a year in a floating zoo. We don't know much about how the family passed the time during that year, except for sending out birds every so often. But whatever Noah's wife did, be it feeding animals or cleaning up after animals or trying to make a home in a pitching, tossing boat, she was a woman who was instrumental in one of the biggest tasks God gave to anyone. (She is also a hero to anyone who has traveled with children and animals!)

Noah didn't dash out of the ark once dry land was spotted. He was patient and waited until God himself told him to come out (Genesis 8:15). At that time, Noah built an altar and sacrificed to the Lord. God was pleased with Noah's actions and, while understanding the evil inclination of man's heart, created a covenant with man that demonstrates his mercy.

A covenant is an agreement or a promise—in this case, between God and man. This was not the first covenant that God had made with man, nor was it the last. In fact, God made a covenant with Adam and Eve in the Garden that he would meet all their needs, and again after the fall in promising a Messiah (Genesis 2:15-16; 3:15). Later, you can read of the covenant he made with Abram through the giving of circumcision (Genesis 15), and the covenant with the people of Israel through the giving of the law (Leviticus and Deuteronomy). The most wonderful covenant is the promise of grace through the giving of God's only son, Jesus. As the writer of Hebrews tells us, "Jesus has become the guarantee of a better covenant" (Hebrews 7:22).

The covenant with Noah promised a regularity of day and night, and of the seasons (Genesis 8:22), a system of justice (Genesis 9:5-6), and a guarantee that the earth would never again be destroyed by a flood (Genesis 9:15). The covenant also stated that Noah's seed was to replenish the earth (Genesis 9:1) and that all fruit and all meat could be eaten for food

(Genesis 9:3). The sign of the covenant was the rainbow.

I must admit, when I see a rainbow I don't check off all the promises and agreements of the covenant that God made with Noah. Rainbows simply remind me that God is merciful. And rainbows remind me that God keeps his promises. If I can remember that, then I will have learned the lessons of Noah, the faithful witness, and the flood. And then I can, in the words of the children's song I referred to earlier, "rise and shine and give God the glory, glory" as a child of the Lord!

The Scriptures are replete with references to God being a witness of people's lives and their treatment of others. As we have seen in this chapter, God also gives us witnesses who attest to his love and faithfulness throughout his Scriptures—witnesses such as death, Enoch, Noah and the rainbow, and many others. The logical response is for us, like Paul, to become his witnesses to the world: "...a witness of what you have seen of me and what I will show you" (Acts 26:16b). From the beginning, God has wanted mankind to know and to love him and to be in intimate relationship with him.

· *Taking It Home* ·

1. How do you feel about discussing death? Does it give you comfort to know that Jesus has experienced it and has been victorious—and that he promises you that same victory? How does death remind you of the realities of life?

2. Enoch walked with God...right up to the door of heaven. Think about your walk with God: When did

---

[2]Genesis 31:50; Judges 11:10; 1 Samuel 12:5, 20:23,42; Romans 1:9; 2 Corinthians 1:23; 1 Thessalonians 2:5

it start? Which times were the paths level and easy to travel? Which times were the hills steep and rocky and difficult to travel? What have you learned about yourself from both? Are you committed to finish the race no matter what?

3. Think about the joy God experienced as he created man and woman in his own image. Then think about the hurt he experienced when they did not trust his love and sinned against him. By the time of Noah, sin was rampant, and God's heart was broken. Does it break your heart when you see people who are lost in their sin? Why should it?

4. As you read the description of Dachau, how did it affect you? Did you block both the information and your emotions, or did you allow the facts to get to your heart? Man has such capacity for evil, but what have you learned about God's power to change us, no matter how sinful we are? What is the work of the Spirit in this process?

5. Noah was faithful to complete the task God had given him. What tasks has God given you? Are you being faithful, day in and day out, to complete those tasks? Do you ask for help and advice to be a better "builder"?

6. When you see a rainbow, does the sight fill your heart with wonder? Do you remember God's promise to Noah? Do you remember some of God's promises to you? The rainbow reminds us that our faithful God will never break a promise.

7. From the beginning, God has wanted mankind to know and to love him and to be in intimate relationship with him. If you have accepted that offer from God, are you now being a reliable witness and getting his message out to the world?

The Wayfarer

5

Genesis
12-22

The LORD had said to Abram, "Leave
your country, your people and your
father's household and go to the land I
will show you.

"I will make you into a great nation
    and I will bless you;
I will make your name great,
    and you will be a blessing.
I will bless those who bless you,
    and whoever curses you I will curse;
and all peoples on earth
    will be blessed through you."

GENESIS 12:1-3

We are only up to the twelfth chapter of Genesis, yet the
earth is filled with people! Even after the devastation of the
flood, the sons of Noah did their part and replenished the
world with their descendants. An unfortunate incident in-
volving a tower (Genesis 11) hastened the scattering of people
throughout the land, and then we are introduced to a family
in the region of Haran who have been called to travel: to
journey to a place that will be called "home."

Come Home

Abram was not originally from Haran, but had traveled there with his father from Ur. Archaeologists have discovered that the city of Ur, found at the southern tip of the Euphrates River, was a civilized center of highly advanced culture. Discoveries of libraries, schools, textbooks, dictionaries and other reference tools confirm that those who were raised there were most likely literate and well educated. Abram was not an ignorant nomad traveling across an ancient land, but an intelligent and wealthy sojourner who had been called by God.

Abram, or "Abraham," as he is later called, is spoken of frequently throughout the Scriptures and has been called by many the "father of faith." (See Romans 4.) Hebrews 11:8-9 affirms him as an example of living by faith:

> *By faith Abraham, when called to go to a place he would later receive as his inheritance, obeyed and went, even though he did not know where he was going. By faith he made his home in the promised land like a stranger in a foreign country....*

He believed that God would bless him as he said he would, even before all things were made clear to him. Even before he left Haran, he understood that his wife Sarai was barren (Genesis 11:30), and yet he accepted by faith that God would make him into a great nation. He is commended for having a trust in God about things unseen and an obedience to go wherever God called him to go.

Steps of Faith

As disciples, we are called to have that kind of "do anything, go anywhere, give up everything" faith. Yet so often we want to see the end result; we want to have all the answers before we set out with great steps of faith. We want to make sure our financial, physical and emotional needs will be met, and we don't want to be "foolish." While it is wise to think things through and make educated decisions, we are ultimately called to leap into the unknown and trust that God will take care of all of our needs.

Abraham's example was especially precious to me when I set out on a mission team to Paris, France. I had never been to France, and my knowledge of the French language was limited to what I had learned in the eighth grade: "Comment allez-vous?" I had two elementary-school-aged children who spoke no French; I didn't know where we would live, and I hardly knew anyone in the whole country of France. Our family had moved quite a bit during the previous two years. I had lived in hotels, rented apartments, in friends' homes, and (it seemed like) in cars and airplanes. But my husband and I were convinced that God would use us in Paris, that we could build up the church there and teach the French people about Jesus. So off we went.

Our first stop upon our arrival was an apartment that had been temporarily rented for us until we could find a permanent place. It was December, very close to Christmastime, and I had settled in my mind that the kids wouldn't have much of a holiday that year—there just wasn't time to prepare. But I wasn't prepared for what God had in store. As we walked into our apartment, my eyes were immediately drawn to a huge Christmas tree in the middle of that tiny room, covered with handmade paper ornaments. Some Christians from the Paris church had purchased the tree for us, and their children had made the decorations. At that point, any doubts about God taking care of us were immediately dispelled! I was convinced that he would meet our needs and would give us friends that would last a lifetime.

Steps of faith don't always involve going to foreign countries. In fact, great steps of faith are often decisions that are

much less exotic, but no less significant. Faith to reach out to
the lost, faith to give of our money, faith to embark on new
relationships, faith to change our character—these are all steps
into the abyss of the unknown. God is always calling us to
these kinds of decisions, and he is always there to bless us
when we obey. God will never disappoint us!

Perhaps you are saying to yourself, "But I *did* step out in
faith and things didn't turn out the way I planned, and I *am*
disappointed." It is true that there are times we make gigantic
faith decisions and we feel disappointed with the results. Maybe
it was the time you took a job thinking it was what God wanted
you to do, and it turned out to be a fiasco. Maybe it was that
boyfriend you were sure was "Mr. Right" but he turned out to
be "Mr. Wrong." Maybe it was the time you poured your energy and heart out to a friend only to have her fall away from
the Lord. If you have ever felt some of these qualms about
trusting in God, then that is precisely why you need to learn
about Abraham and Sarah. Things didn't always go the way
they planned it, either, and they made some grievous errors
when they felt disappointed. But in the end, you will agree
that trusting in God, even when it seems unreasonable, is the
only way to go.

The Promise

God's promise to Abraham that all the families of the
earth would be blessed through him is also a promise to us.
Because of Abraham's faith, my family is blessed and so is
yours. Why? Because it was through Abraham that eventually
Jesus, the Christ, came into this world. As Christians, we are
by faith Abraham's children, and we share in God's promises
to him. When Abraham obeyed, it is doubtful that he realized the scope of the consequences: the multitudes of people
who would be grateful for his obedience. But I am grateful,
and I am also encouraged to know that others may be blessed

by my obedience as well. Abraham, my "father of faith" changed my life because of his obedience thousands of years ago, and I strive to follow his example today.

I may never know the effect my obedience will have on others. My goals during our time in France naturally included helping to convert French women. I knew I needed to reach out to the Americans in my French class as well, but did not really see that as a major focus in my life. One of the women from that class, whom I studied with and converted, eventually moved back to the midwestern United States and has had an incredible impact there. Each time I receive a letter from her, she tells me of new people that she was able to reach out to and baptize. It is so encouraging to realize that God used me to make an impact on people whom I probably will never even meet—until we meet in heaven.

The Other Woman

> *Now Sarai, Abram's wife, had borne him no children. But she had an Egyptian maidservant named Hagar; so she said to Abram, "The LORD has kept me from having children. Go, sleep with my maidservant; perhaps I can build a family through her."*
>
> *Abram agreed to what Sarai said. So after Abram had been living in Canaan ten years, Sarai his wife took her Egyptian maidservant Hagar and gave her to her husband to be his wife. He slept with Hagar, and she conceived"* (Genesis 16:1-4a).

Somehow, the words from the scripture above sound familiar, don't they? They bring to mind the words found in Genesis 3:6b: "She also gave some to her husband, who was with her, and he ate it." Sarai, like Eve, was taken with an idea that seemed right to her and convinced her husband to go along with the plan.

Let's get a clear picture of Sarai and Abram's predicament: They had been through a lot together. They had traveled to foreign lands, endured a famine, faced danger in Egypt and succumbed to the temptation to lie, worked to resolve conflict with relatives, and defeated some neighboring kings in a war. (Read Genesis 12-14.) The child that God had promised was way past due, and Sarai's biological clock had stopped ticking long before. Furthermore, the customs of the time would find Sarai's idea perfectly reasonable: a barren wife should provide a way for her husband to have heirs. In summary, Sarai and Abram had a lot of rough times waiting for this child of promise, and now to them, it was time to take matters into their own hands.

This all seems perfectly reasonable from a human point of view, as I'm sure it did to the childless couple. Sadly, God was left out of the equation. God had chosen Sarai, not Hagar, to have Abraham's child. God would act with his best timing, not at their convenience. God wanted things done his way, not the world's way. What seemed to be a simple solution to their problem became an explosion of conflict.

Hagar had probably been Sarai's favorite maidservant. Most likely she had been acquired in Egypt during the famine and had been elevated to her high position due to her respect for and obedience to her mistress. As Sarai pondered over her predicament, Hagar must have come to mind. As painful as it must have been to give another woman to her husband, Sarai must have assumed that Hagar would continue to be loyal and trustworthy, and everything would work out in the end.

But that's not what happened. As soon as Hagar learned that she was pregnant, she became haughty and prideful and despised her mistress. She probably mocked Sarai, and may have even taunted her about her infertility. Quite possibly, Hagar assured herself that now that she carried the master's child, no harm could come to her.

Sarai turned her problems on her husband. She blamed him for the unfortunate turn of events and asked him to choose between her and the mother of his child. What a soap opera this had become! Sarai had completely disregarded all the plans and promises of God. Abram's response was to throw up his hands. "You take care of it," he, in essence, declared. "I'm outta here!"

Sarai's intense mistreatment of Hagar drove her to run away. Then God "found" her, corrected her and comforted her. The "other woman" was told to behave herself and that God would take care of her and her unborn child. Though Hagar returned that time, several years later, she and her son were sent away, and again God cared for them and promised them a future. Twice Hagar faced death, and twice Hagar was confronted with God, who cared for her all along. Hagar had to realize that she was not entirely blameless in her troubled situation; her sin was exposed as clearly as Sarai's. She was directed to change, to trust in God, and to look to him for protection.

Taking Things into Our Own Hands

Many women today can sympathize with the cruelty that Hagar endured and the insecurity that she felt. Single mothers and women who are abused or abandoned find a soft spot in their heart for her because they can relate so well to her despair. What all women must remember is what Hagar learned about God: "You are the God who sees me" (Genesis 16:13). They must remember that God sees and knows and cares.

There are so many situations in which we are tempted to take things into our own hands, to do what seems right to us. Married women whose husbands are emotionally distant are tempted to get even—to seek attention from other men, or simply to pull away emotionally themselves. Mothers with children who are being overlooked by teachers or others in authority are tempted to break the rules to push their child ahead. Career women, working hard to make ends meet, are tempted to let some family needs go unattended to make just a little more money. Wives who have been hurt by their husbands are tempted to make derogatory statements to their children or friends—anything that will make their husbands look bad and make them look a little better. Single women who assumed they would have married years earlier are tempted to make themselves available to men who are not Christians, and then they find themselves with a husband who has little interest in serving God.

The solutions that we come up with seem reasonable, and maybe the methods are the same as some of those employed by our friends or family, but if they are not God's solutions found in the Bible, the result will be chaos. The world tells women today to get even, to fight back, to be aggressive. I am all for assertiveness, but we must be women who assert forgiveness, kindness, compassion and trust. These are not weak, wimpy qualities, but are qualities that require strength.

Sarai, Abram and Hagar all made grave mistakes and they suffered the devastating consequences. Not only they, but mankind for generations to come would suffer because of the animosity that developed between the future descendants of Hagar and Sarai. Their sin caused incredible damage. In spite of this, God worked to bring about the results that he wanted. God can work with us in spite of our mistakes as long as we are willing to change and to trust in him again. We must resolve to live our lives his way, according to his Word. Only then will his promises to us be fully realized!

Pleading with God

> *Then Abraham spoke up again: "Now that I have been so bold as to speak to the Lord, though I am nothing but dust and ashes..." (Genesis 18:27).*

Abram was a man of faith, in spite of his frailties and weaknesses. Following the episode with Hagar, Abram was given the covenant of circumcision and his name was changed from "Abram" to "Abraham" (meaning "father of many"). Sarai's name was also changed; she became "Sarah" (meaning "princess"). The promise that a son would be born to them was again given, and it elicited Sarah's laughter–after all, she was ninety years old at the time! Sarah and Abraham were refreshed to be reminded that nothing is too hard for the Lord (Genesis 18:14).

That strengthening from God set the stage for Abraham to come to God with some grave concerns. He had been in-formed that Sodom and Gomorrah were about to be destroyed, and it caused him great distress. His own nephew, Lot, had chosen years before to make his home in that area (Genesis 13). While Lot's greed and worldliness must have been a source of concern to Abraham, he obviously loved his relative dearly and continued to see the best in him. Abraham came before God, eventually reasoning with him not to destroy the city if there were at least ten righteous persons there.

Abraham's interaction with the Lord is a powerful por-trayal of God's loving willingness to hear us out. Abraham had to be bold to speak to God, but he had to temper that boldness with complete respect, humility and submission. Abraham never doubted who was in control. His prayer was not to change God's mind about justice, but to ask God to be merciful in the midst of his judgment.

God wants us to be real with him, to reason with him and to pour out our hearts. Jesus himself commended a Canaanite woman who logically appealed to him (Matthew 15:27), and he also taught about persistence in prayer (Luke 18:7). Before we became disciples, for many of us, prayers, if we said them at all, were prayers we had memorized in childhood. Or per-haps we were taught to pray, "God bless him and God bless her..." and that's about as deep as it went! I've spoken to many women who had extreme views on personal prayer. Some were convinced that they should never pray for themselves, because they were taught that it was selfish to do so. There are also those who refused to pray for anything unless it was really *big*, because they believed God couldn't be bothered with the little things! I'm grateful for Philippians 4:6 which nullifies both of those opinions: "Do not be anxious about anything, but in *everything*, by prayer and petition, with thanksgiving, present your requests to God" (emphasis added).

The biggest faith challenge for me personally is to pray when things seem hopeless. I went through this dilemma recently when I studied the Bible with a young woman whom I loved dearly and for whom I had prayed for years. After an initial conviction that she needed to become a disciple and to be baptized, family pressures and false teachings confused her enough to cause her to turn away from the truth of God's word. I was devastated, even to the point of not wanting to pray! I felt as though God had not answered my prayers for her, so why keep on praying? After grieving for some time and being comforted by God through the help of disciples, I finally repented. I continue to pray for this woman, as well as for others whom I am reaching out to. I know that my persistence in prayer is crucial to helping these people find God. I want to follow Abraham's example of offering pleading, consistent prayers to God for others to be saved. Just as he is known as the "father of faith," so I want to be known as a "woman of faith."

Abraham had certainly learned the lesson that God does things in his own time. We must ask ourselves if there are issues that we have given up on, things that we've stopped praying about: a husband who has yet to become a Christian, a child who has seemed to lose faith in God, or a dream that has never come to fruition. Whatever may have caused you to lose faith, be strengthened by God's promise to bless you and guide you as you seek to regain faith in him. Approach him boldly, but humbly. He wants to hear from you again.

Don't Look Back!

> *"Flee for your lives! Don't look back, and don't stop anywhere in the plain! Flee to the mountains or you will be swept away!" (Genesis 19:17).*

The citizens of Sodom and Gomorrah were incredibly wicked. Lot, though he was weak, was still morally upright enough to insist that the two men he met (who were actually angels) should come to spend the night at his house, rather than in the unprotected square. (Read Genesis 19 to get the full story.) As they finished dinner, they realized that all the men in the city had gathered around Lot's house, hoping to have sex with the two visitors. The Bible says, "all the men...both young and old" (Genesis 19:4).

Lot's response to the men of the city was bizarre. He offered his own daughters to them instead! Whether he thought they would lose interest and go away or whether he actually was willing to give his daughters to be raped by these men is a mystery to me. Whatever the case, this whole episode shows the evil that was there—the complete lack of moral decency that had corroded the character of all the people. The angels protected Lot and his household, and hurried them out of the doomed city because God had not even been able to find ten righteous people there (per the agreement with Abraham).

The moral decay that pervaded the city unfortunately pervaded the family of Lot as well. Lot's wife longed to see the sinful place she had left behind and was turned into a pillar of salt (Genesis 19:26). Much later, the daughters of Lot manipulated their own father into having sex with them so that they could have children (Genesis 19:36). Their actions were not initiated so much out of lust, but rather out of desperation. (After all, isn't desperation the reason many women succumb to immorality?)

Looking back, we can see that Lot's mistakes in life began with his initial choice to live near Sodom. His decision was based on the beauty of the area and the lucrative business he could do there. As time passed, he got closer and closer to the city, and closer and closer to the sin, which was already well known (Genesis 13:13). He was foolish if he thought that the wickedness of his environment would not invade his own household. Although he was saved due to Abraham's intercession and God's mercy, his life was marred by failure.

Making Spiritual Choices

In the same way today, many people's mistakes are brought about by poor choices. Our choices in life must not be based on the best jobs, the most money, the best schools, the prettiest neighborhoods or the most comfortable communities. We must make choices that are going to be best for us spiritually, not materially. Our decisions must be weighed in light of finding the circumstances that will bring out the best in our families, and will bring them closer to God. I'm inspired by parents who will sell their homes and move to be a part of a church where they believe their teenagers' spiritual needs will be met. I'm encouraged by fathers who will take lower paying jobs because they have the conviction that their families need them more than they need extra money. I'm refreshed by couples who refuse promotions because they believe that a move is not best for building up the kingdom of God. I have known people who have made each of these choices. I believe that Lot would look at people like them with admiration and would say to them, "I wish I had done that!"

And what about Lot's wife? Here was a woman who did not appreciate the salvation she was receiving. She was running away from total annihilation; she had a second chance, along with her family, and a guarantee of safety. Yet, she looked back. It's appalling to see women who have become disciples, who have received that "second chance," and yet have turned back to a life devoid of God. In spite of warnings, these women take their eyes off Jesus and long for the familiar, even if it only promises destruction.

But in a subtle way, many disciples look back in ways they may not even realize. Maybe they long for an easier life, one which does not require them to take up the cross of Jesus. Maybe they want to simply fit in with the crowd. Maybe they want to trust in their own ways, and not rely on God and his wisdom. This is how we lived before we knew God. Do we look back? Or are we fleeing from that life?

The Test

> *"Take your son, your only son, Isaac, whom you love, and go to the region of Moriah. Sacrifice him there as a burnt offering..." (Genesis 22:2).*

Just when we have let out a sigh of relief because Abraham and Sarah's child has been born, God surprises us by presenting another monumental challenge to this family. Sarah named her beautiful baby boy Isaac and was overjoyed that God had allowed her, a woman in her nineties, to bear a child. And Abraham, who had "faced the fact that his body was as good as dead...and that Sarah's womb was also dead...was strengthened in his faith and gave glory to God" (Romans 4:19-20). But soon, the test that God would present to Abraham was one that could build up his faith, or could crush his faith forever.

Once again, God asks a faithful follower to do the unimaginable. According to the laws of God, killing another human being was wrong (Genesis 9:6). In addition, God had promised Abraham that Isaac would be the one through whom all his descendants would come. How could God ask him to sacrifice his beloved, promised son?

Abraham did not know the answer to that question, but what he did know was that he was called to obedience. And because of his trust in God, he was willing to do whatever God asked of him, even when it hurt beyond words. This is the lesson we must learn from God's command to sacrifice Isaac. It is so simple to trust and obey when we agree with the commands of God. I can wholeheartedly agree that it's best and right to love, to forgive, to rejoice, to share, to avoid sinful conduct, etc. But there are times when the commands of God are really tough: sacrifice, love your enemies, accept persecution, deny yourself. Those are the commands that are harder to obey. But Abraham knew that if he was to obey God, he had to obey everything and not simply pick and choose what he wanted to do. If God called Abraham to give up what he held most dear in life, that was exactly what he was going to do.

By the time God presented his challenge, Isaac was a young boy, capable of carrying wood and asking questions of his father. The questions must have cut Abraham deeply as he assured the boy that God himself would provide the sacrifice. And it is certain that he understood what was happening as his father bound him and raised the knife to kill him. But the Scriptures do not reveal any struggling or fear on the boy's part—perhaps the peace and trust that his father exhibited had a calming effect on him. Then, just as he was about to plunge the knife into the boy, an angel of the Lord called out to stop him from going through with the deed. God did indeed provide an animal to be sacrificed, and Abraham and his young son returned home, with the blessings and commendation of God and with a purified faith.

Lest you struggle with an attitude toward God, the testing of Abraham was not an exercise given to watch him squirm.

The test was not simply to prove to God that he was devoted, but also to prove it to himself. Abraham, even after years of following God, still had to make leaps of faith. As we grow older, the tendency to grow attached to the things of this world can get stronger. We must continually be willing to give back to God the blessings he has given to us. As a college student, it was a rather easy thing to say, "I will love God more than my husband, more than my children"—the simple reason was that I didn't have a husband or children! Once I was married, and then again after my children came along, I had to reassess my commitment to God. I had to resolve that God still came first in my heart. As the years go on, new things, places and people enter the picture that endear themselves to me; again and again I must decide that God is number one.

"Family" is precious to all of us. It tears our heart when decisions must be made that take us away from relatives whom we love dearly. Yet it is impressive to consider the Christians who have left home and family for the sake of the gospel, and to see how God has blessed those decisions. I can think of several people who have traveled to distant lands to preach the gospel, yet their prayers and their example have influenced the family they left behind to become disciples.

"Money" is another precious commodity, whether we like to admit it or not. But when we give sacrificially, God has a way of making it up in more ways than we can count. A childless couple in Boston, who had been saving money to adopt a child, decided to donate those funds in order that mission teams could be sent out around the world. When their prospective child was ready to be adopted, they did not have the financial means to make it happen. They realized, though, that they could not out-give God. Money became available in unexpected ways, and now they are the proud parents of not one, but two beautiful adopted children.

God's Unselfish Sacrifice

Even the sacrifice that Abraham was willing to make does not compare to the sacrifice God made in letting his Son die for me. God's heart could hurt for the pain that Abraham felt because he, too, had to offer up his Son, his only Son, whom he loved. In that case, God did not stop the killing, but allowed it to happen so that Jesus' death could be the substitute for the punishment I personally deserve for my sins.

Abraham passed the test of faith in the way he lived his life. He followed, obeyed, trusted and sacrificed. God is testing all of us in the same way today. He is calling us to trust him and to entrust to him everything in our lives. Wherever you are in response to this testing, look to Abraham, the father of our faith, and be encouraged to live every day by faith. God is longing to bless you!

· Taking It Home ·

1. Abraham is certainly an example of one who was willing to go anywhere, do anything and give up everything. Think of examples of your willingness to do the same.

2. Do you trust that if you sacrifice for God, then he will meet your needs? How do you distinguish between "wants" and "needs"?

3. In which situations have you taken matters into your own hands in an effort to make things go the way you think they should go? What was the result?

4. Abraham was a man who was willing to appeal to God for the welfare of those he loved. How much do you appeal to the Lord for the lost? Do you keep asking God to save the souls of your family, your

friends, your neighbors? Do you pray specifically and reason with God? Do you keep on praying even when it seems like a lost cause? Will someone be saved from hell because of your prayers? How do you specifically want to be more like Abraham in this area?

5. In what ways are you tempted to "look back" longingly at your old life? How does Satan want to deceive you? How will you keep a godly perspective and keep moving ahead spiritually?

6. God tested Abraham's faith by calling him to sacrifice Isaac. What kind of grade are you getting on the test of your faith? Would Abraham say you are barely making the grade, failing miserably or passing? Remember that without God's mercy and grace, none of us could pass the test.

The
Welcoming

6

Genesis
24

*Abraham was now old and well advanced in years,
and the LORD had blessed him in every way. He said
to the chief servant in his household, the one in charge
of all that he had, "Put your hand under my thigh.
I want you to swear by the LORD, the God of heaven
and the God of earth, that you will not get a wife for
my son from the daughters of the Canaanites, among
whom I am living, but will go to my country and my
own relatives and get a wife for my son Isaac."*

GENESIS 24:1-4

It's amazing how your perspective changes as you get older.
As a young girl, the thought of arranged marriages was horrifying! Imagine having your mom and dad pick out your future
husband. My parents had a phrase for certain boys that I dated:
"He's a right nice young man." When I heard that, my teenage
rebellion automatically kicked in. It was time to break off that
relationship!

Now, as the mother of two teenagers who will be facing
decisions to marry sometime in the next few decades (!), I've
become quite fond of the idea of arranged marriages. Certainly their father and I understand what's best for them and
who would make the best match. We could find someone with
a compatible family background, someone *we* get along with

well, and surely they would make a perfect couple. I'm sure my offspring would be so pleased and thankful for my help!

Calm down. I'm only joking! While I do think it is wise for parents to guide their children in finding the right spouse, I'm quite willing to let mine do the choosing themselves. Parents have hopefully raised their children to make this decision carefully and wisely, so that when the time comes, they can be fully trusted in the choice they make.

A Marriage Made for Heaven

Customs were different in Abraham's time, and arranged marriages were quite the norm. Marriages were not usually based on "falling in love," but on political alliances, land agreements and family connections. (Of course, there are many places in the world today where this is still the case.) Abraham's problem was compounded by the fact that he desired for Isaac to marry a godly woman who would be a partner with him in the covenant of promise. It was imperative that the right woman be found.

It is often said that deciding who to marry is the second most important decision in your life. The most important decision is, of course, the decision to become a Christian and to follow Jesus for the rest of your life. The second decision will either support that decision, or eventually erode it. When you marry, you are uniting heart, soul, mind and body with another human being for life. Your choice of who to marry may very well determine where you spend eternity.

After becoming a Christian, there were some fellows whom I had previously dated who couldn't understand why I refused to keep on going out with them. But I knew that my goals in life had completely changed and that I only wanted to date men who loved God wholeheartedly. I tried to explain this to them, and in fact, one former boyfriend came to church and did become a Christian. (We did not date again, but remained friends.) As a disciple, it was wonderful to begin going out on dates with men whom I could trust, men who would respect me and not try to take advantage of me. During this time I met Randall McKean, the man I would ultimately marry. I fell in love, partly because he was *so* good-looking and *so* smart and *so* romantic, but mostly because I saw in him a deep love for God and a strength that I knew I could rely upon. I know the decision I made to marry him has been a major reason why I have stayed faithful to God to this day. He has encouraged me and guided our family to serve God and give our best for Jesus over the years. Our marriage was made *on* earth, but it was made *for* heaven. (By the way, my parents wholeheartedly approved of him, and this time, when they called him a "right nice young man," I thoroughly agreed!)

Mission Possible

The man entrusted with the task of finding Isaac a wife, who simply said of himself, "I am Abraham's servant" (Genesis 24:34), was most likely Eliezer of Damascus. Before Isaac was born, Abraham had been willing to let Eliezer be the one who would inherit his estate (Genesis 15:2). Eliezer could have regarded Isaac as the son who displaced him and could have wished for harm to come to him. But his faithfulness to Abraham extended to Abraham's son, and he welcomed the opportunity to take on a task that would bring blessings to his master. (Read Genesis 24 to get the full story.)

Placing his hand under the thigh of Abraham was the sign of an oath. It signified an agreement that would not be revoked and showed the seriousness of the promise. The servant was cautioned not to take Isaac away from the land of promise, but to bring the woman to him. Eliezer immediately packed up and went on his journey, a distance of about 500 miles, partly through the desert. When he arrived in the city of Nahor, his first act was to go to the well and pray to meet the girl who would be just right for Isaac. When he saw that God had answered his prayer, he did not hesitate to speak to her family, to tell them his mission, and to arrange to return immediately to his master with the girl. He wanted no delays and told the family, "Do not detain me, now that the Lord has granted success to my journey. Send me on my way so I may go to my master" (Genesis 24:56).

Abraham's servant was urgent, but he was not frantic. He planned, he prayed and he acted. He understood that the best way to please his master was to do his job well and to do it quickly.

All of us are given jobs to do. Our husbands, our church leaders, our friends are constantly calling upon us to run errands, to make phone calls, to accomplish tasks both large and small. Often, these "jobs" may appear to have no benefit to us personally, but are necessary favors that we do for others. Is our attitude like that of Abraham's servant? Or do we "forget" to pick up the dry-cleaning? Do we put off those phone calls? Do we neglect to write that letter? Do we find the statement: "Oops! I forgot, but I'll do it tomorrow," frequently on our lips?

During a time when I was feeling that my children were not being diligent to follow directions, I read to them Proverbs 10:26: "As vinegar to the teeth and smoke to the eyes, so is a sluggard to those who send him." I demonstrated this verse by putting vinegar on a piece of bread and letting them take a bite. I lit a match and waved a little smoke toward their eyes. They sensed the unpleasantness, and I reiterated the scripture by saying, "When I ask you to do things, and you dawdle and piddle and don't get it done, this is how it makes me feel!" In contrast, I read Proverbs 25:13: "Like the coolness of snow at harvest time is a trustworthy messenger to those who send him; he refreshes the spirit of his masters." In New England, we have no absence of snow, and I reminded the kids of how pleasant the first snow of the year is. The descriptions helped them to understand the importance of doing quickly and well what they have been asked to do.

When I was a child, I often complained about the chores my mother would ask me to do. Her requests for me to set the table, to do the dishes, or to clean my room were met with mutterings of "Do I have to?" My father, overhearing my grumbling, took me aside and gave me the script of how I was supposed to respond to my mother's requests. "Just say, 'I'd be *delighted!*'" he told me. My standard answer around the house did become "I'd be delighted!" although at times I said it with a growl. But I did learn that how we respond to requests makes a big difference in our own hearts and in our relationships with those who are asking.

It's hard enough for some people to ask for favors; it's even harder when their requests are met with hesitation or resistance. For example, when my children were younger, it was a bit difficult for me to ask for baby-sitters. I knew that those I asked had things to do, and I didn't want to burden anyone by asking for help. Imagine how painful it was if the answer came back: "We-e-ll, I *guess* I could—I was hoping to stay home and rest that night, but I suppose I should help you instead." In contrast, imagine how pleased I was when the response was: "I'd love to take care of your children—thanks for asking me!"

We all have many missions every day of our lives. I've tried to make it a habit that when someone asks, "Can you do me a favor?" the words I say, with a smile and with enthusiasm, are "Sure, I'd love to help!" We must make sure that in all we do, we respond with eagerness, with prayer and with efficiency, as Eliezar did. Our attitude can make all the difference to those we serve, so let's serve gladly in all that we do!

For Better or For Worse

> *Rebekah also looked up and saw Isaac. She got
> down from her camel and asked the servant, "Who is
> that man in the field coming to meet us?"*
>
> *"He is my master," the servant answered. So she
> took her veil and covered herself.*
>
> *Then the servant told Isaac all he had done. Isaac
> brought her into the tent of his mother Sarah, and he
> married Rebekah. So she became his wife, and he loved
> her; and Isaac was comforted after his mother's death"*
> *(Genesis 24:64-67).*

Eliezer had been the recipient of Rebekah's welcoming service in Nahor when she had given him water to drink and had
offered to water his camels as well. She had also offered him
hospitality in her father's home. Furthermore, she displayed
an eagerness to submit to God's plan for her life when she
told her family, after being given the choice of leaving right
away or delaying the trip, "I will go" (Genesis 24:58). These
thoughtful qualities must have radiated in the presence of her
husband, endearing her to him right from the start.

There is an incredible tenderness that is evident in the
relationship between Isaac and Rebekah. Even though they
had never seen one another before, Isaac loved her and was
comforted by her. As time went on and Rebekah was found to
be barren, Isaac "prayed to the Lord on behalf of his wife"
(Genesis 25:21). Their affection was also obvious years later
when Isaac and Rebekah had traveled to Gerar due to a famine, and gave in to the same deception that had occurred with
Isaac's parents: He pretended that Rebekah was not his wife,
but was caught caressing (some translations say "fondling")
her (Genesis 26:8).

Love, comfort, prayer, physical affection—these are marks
of a close and intimate relationship. They were a close couple,

brought together by God and a loving family. They had been promised numerous descendants and lands and blessings. They were granted success everywhere they turned. But something went terribly wrong. Before her life was over, Rebekah would find herself alienated from her husband and estranged from both her sons.

One of the most heartbreaking things to see is a marriage that has gone sour—a couple that starts off with promises and kisses and stars in their eyes, and ends up with bitterness and hostility and divorce. Rebekah's life demonstrated character flaws that were heavily to blame in the breakdown of her marriage, as we will see.

Competition, Manipulation, Domination

While Rebekah and Isaac were not necessarily guilty of competing with each other, they were competing through their children. Isaac's favorite was Esau; Rebekah's favorite was Jacob. The favoritism that was rampant in this family was not only incredibly devastating to the boys, but had a corrosive effect on the parents' relationship as well. It caused Isaac and Rebekah to be on different teams. Rebekah wanted to do whatever it would take to make sure that *her* favorite was the one who would receive the blessings. God had already promised that Jacob would be the stronger of the two boys, but she wanted to make sure it would happen, so she took action.

Rebekah's assertiveness and sensitivity to others' needs had already been demonstrated. At this point in her life, she used these very qualities in a scheme that would undermine her whole family. What had been Rebekah's greatest strengths now became her greatest weaknesses. She deviously prepared food that she knew Isaac would enjoy, dressed Jacob in Esau's clothes, covered him so that he would appear more hairy, and sent him in to her husband to steal the blessing from her older son.

Even when Jacob was hesitant to go through with the plan, she pushed and bullied him into going along with her. "Now, my son, listen carefully and do what I tell you....Just do what I say" (Genesis 27:8,13). She used those same words later when she discovered that Esau was seeking revenge. She manipulated Isaac into sending Jacob away by complaining about Esau's wives and insisting that Jacob take a wife from the family lineage. She wrongfully assumed that Jacob would be able to return quickly and that the whole incident would be forgotten, but apparently that is the last time she ever saw her beloved younger son.

Samples of competition, manipulation and domination abound in families today. In case you are not sure if you are following in Rebekah's footsteps, ask yourself the following questions:

- Do you show favoritism to one child over another? Is one child the "good one" in your heart?
- When your child exhibits flaws in his or her life, do you pronounce, "You're just like your father"?
- Do you frequently remind your husband about mistakes he has made? Is the phrase, "I told you so" on your lips, or even in your heart?
- Do you compare yourself to your husband, trying to "one-up" him on issues like who makes more money, who has the better job, or who is affirmed publicly more often? Do you find yourself jealous of his recognition or honors?
- Do you confide in your children about things you won't tell your husband? Do you ask them to keep secrets from their father?
- Do you cry, pout, whine or sulk to get your way?
- Does your family have to "tread softly" because they don't know how you might react?

- Do you withhold sex to get even with your husband for various offenses? Do you initiate sex only when he has lived up to your expectations?
- Do you "fight dirty" by bringing up irrelevant issues? Are you constantly reminding your family of how they have hurt you in the past?
- Do you tell only part of the story to convince your husband to agree with your side?
- Do you yell, slam doors or use any kind of unrestrained physical force with your family?

These questions must be answered carefully to ascertain whether or not we are living in the shadow of Rebekah. Not only married women with children must evaluate these issues, but any woman who shares a home with others. Our living situations may differ depending on our circumstances in life, but the challenges are all very similar. Living in that apartment with three other young women before I married was an education for me! Sharing the bathroom, paying the bills, keeping the place clean, coordinating schedules—all of these issues were potential sources of conflict. I had to *learn* how to live with others. I had to deal with things in my personality and character that made *me* hard to live with at times. Things that were insignificant to me might be things that really bugged my roommates. For example, one of my roommates couldn't stand the fact that I slept with my earrings on at night. For her, sleeping with earrings on was so uncomfortable that even looking at me dozing peacefully with my earrings firmly fastened in my ears drove her crazy! I couldn't understand it, but to appease her I began to remove my earrings before I hit the pillow. I could sleep perfectly well whether my earrings were in or out, but it taught me to become a woman who was willing to do the little things for those with whom I shared my home. Any living situation can bring out the best or the worst in a person. (My current "roommate," my husband, doesn't mind my earrings at all!)

For Good or Evil

The qualities that we admire most about Rebekah had not been lost, but had been misdirected. Just like Rebekah, we can use our talents and abilities for good or for evil. Maybe you are someone who is particularly sensitive to others' needs. Great! Then you can be empathetic and warm, and make people feel special by understanding them so well. Or, you could become manipulative—reading people so well that you know exactly what buttons to push to hurt them or what to say to get them to respond as you would prefer.

Perhaps your strength is your courageous and adventurous spirit! That could lead you to become strong, submissive and determined to do God's will. On the other hand, you might develop stubbornness and independence, always demanding things to go your way.

Are you a person who loves to serve others? Then you are probably concerned and giving, expecting nothing in return. But you also might be manipulative, making others depend on you and waiting for thanks or some form of payment.

How we use all of our strengths is up to each one of us.

Building Your Home

Proverbs 14:1 says, "The wise woman builds her house, but with her own hands the foolish one tears hers down." Rebekah was wise when she started out. She was courageous, thoughtful and kind. As far as we can tell, the foundation of her marriage was solid. Yet along the way, she began to tear her house down. She neglected to build. Building a home, like building a house, is accomplished a little at a time. Building your home means making the time to connect with all of your children. Building your home means going after intimacy with your husband in the midst of a busy and hectic schedule. Building your home means praying together and looking to God to accomplish his plans in his ways.

Sometimes the McKean home seems to be pulled in four directions at once. My husband might be meeting with a mission team in the basement, while my daughter is asking to use the car, my son is practicing his drums, and I'm trying to put groceries away. In the midst of all this, the dog is barking and the phone is ringing. For us, building our home means making sure we have time together to reconnect. Before the kids go to school each morning, we discuss the schedule for the day while they are eating their breakfast. We try to have family dinners together each evening to give us time to catch up with one another on the day's activities. We have weekly family devotionals and "discipling" times. My husband and I make sure we have time regularly to talk about our own needs and goals. We pray together every night, and plan special, candle-lit romantic dates in the bedroom. If we don't make time for these kinds of things, we could easily become detached from one another and lead completely separate lives.

Rebekah was not so different from many women today. She had a husband whom she had at least at one point loved. She was ambitious for her children. She felt drawn to one child more than the other. She was willing to do anything to see her child succeed. But when she took things into her own hands, she failed miserably. Among the last words that Scripture quotes her saying are: "I'm disgusted with living" (Genesis 27:46). Here was a woman who welcomed life with gusto, but closed out her life in bitterness and heartache.

While millions of women may not use those words, they close out their lives with a similar sentiment. Somewhere along the way, they allow their lives to get out of control. But we must avoid Rebekah's mistakes and welcome *God's* will for our lives.

· *Taking It Home* ·

1. If you are a parent, no matter how old your child is, you have thought about who he or she will marry someday (if he or she is not already married). Does this thought bring you any temptation to be anxious? To fear that he or she will not make the right choice or that someone will deceive your child? Even though you will not have the right to arrange a marriage for your child as Abraham did, what can you be doing to help him or her to make a wise choice?

2. Since we know that there will be no marriage in heaven, what does the phrase "a marriage made for heaven" mean to you? If you are single, how can you prepare for such a marriage? If you are already married, how can you do your part to help your marriage to be one made for heaven?

3. Abraham's servant was urgent and efficient in following through with the task he was given. How urgent and diligent are you when you have agreed to do something for someone? What does it communicate to the other person when you forget, put it off or even do it in a way different than you were asked to do it?

4. Have you ever experienced favoritism in your family setting? How did it affect you? If you currently have a family of your own, how do you guard against showing favoritism?

5. We have seen that Rebekah was competitive, manipulative and domineering. Which of these three is the greatest temptation for you? How do you ensure that you will continue to overcome in this area?

6. In which life situations have you tried to "take things into your own hands"? What were the results? What conviction do you now have about letting God work out everything within his time frame?

7. Look back over the questions on pages 104 and 105. How many "yeses" did you have? The more yeses, the more need to change.

8. What is one strength you have that can also offer a temptation to sin?

9. Whether you live with friends or family, what are you doing to build your home?

The
Wrestler

7

Genesis
25, 27-33

The Lord said to her,

"Two nations are in your womb,
 and two peoples from within you will be separated;
one people will be stronger than the other,
 and the older will serve the younger."

GENESIS 25:23

Rebekah was experiencing a difficult pregnancy. "The babies jostled each other within her, and she said, 'Why is this happening to me?' So she went to inquire of the Lord" (Genesis 25:22). If the technological miracle of ultrasound had been around in Rebekah's day, she would have discovered that the "jostling" inside of her was because she carried twins. Instead of hearing from a white-coated medical doctor, she heard from God himself. What a sense of wonder must have enveloped her. What a sense of shock must have overwhelmed her. From *no* baby to *two* babies in nine short months or less.

The Twins

Twin children are typically so adorable because of their similarity. Mothers of these twins often add to their "cuteness" by dressing them the same, and it's humorous to watch people try to tell them apart. Sometimes twins are so bonded that they speak their own language, and can tell what the other is thinking. There is a connection between them that is mysterious, even to their parents.

Jacob and Esau certainly were not identical twins. Their physical differences were only the beginning of their dissimilarity. Esau had a fiery complexion and was hairy, while Jacob was smooth. Obviously, you wouldn't have a hard time discerning who was who. As they grew up, Esau became a skillful hunter, loving the outdoors. He was your typical man's man—probably boisterous, full of life, impulsive, tough. I can imagine him thundering across the fields, spear in hand, yelling ferociously as he chased down some hapless animal, then victoriously carrying the bloody carcass back to camp and proudly plopping it down at his father's feet.

On the other hand, Jacob was a man who preferred to remain near the camp—quiet, sensitive and a mama's boy. A good kid who never got into trouble, who stayed clean, came in early and said all the right things. But perhaps he left others unsettled because they never knew what thoughts were churning around in his head.

As if the natural differences weren't enough to cause problems with Jacob and Esau, they had parents who exacerbated the dilemma with their foolish favoritism. The kids had little chance for a close, protective and intimate sibling relationship. As the boys grew, so did the jealousy and competition between them. The real turmoil began over a bowl of stew.

Esau, entering the camp one day, was lured by the delicious aroma of a stew of lentils that Jacob had prepared. His exaggerated desire for food brought out the con artist in his brother, who took advantage of Esau in one of his weak moments. This was the opportunity for Jacob, who intuitively understood Esau's impetuous appetites, to greedily usurp the birthright from his older brother. (A "birthright" was the claim of the oldest son in a family to the largest portion of the inheritance and to the rights and privileges of head of the family upon the death of the father.) Bargaining for the meal with his birthright, Esau revealed an utter disregard for his own future. Meanwhile, Jacob craftily obtained by his own devices what could have been a free gift from God.

Esau's sins were loud, obvious, clearly evident for all to see. He was impulsive, he had no self-control and he gave in to his appetites. Jacob's sins were quiet, insidious, subtle. The difference in character between the two brothers vividly reminds me of a passage from the New Testament: "The sins of some men are obvious, reaching the place of judgment ahead of them; the sins of others trail behind them" (1 Timothy 5:24). This is especially evident in siblings who may be unfortunately labeled, "the good one," and "the bad one." The bad one is always getting into scrapes, is always too loud or too clumsy, has troubles at school, says all the wrong things and causes parents to throw up their hands in despair. The good one has perfect manners, never causes any problems, and captures the admiration of teachers and baby-sitters because of his good behavior. This one says all the right things and is a source of pride to mom and dad. In fact, this child is so well behaved that parents might assume that all is well, and neglect to really find out what is going on below the surface. What one may discover with time, however, is that within the "good one," all kinds of storms are brewing. This child may be full of trouble, even though the trouble might not be quite so conspicuous.

Grown-Up Truth

What is true for children is also true for adults. Some women's sins are obvious—immorality, drunkenness, fits of rage, etc. But there are others who come across as perfect ladies who, in actuality, are living lives of secret sin. They smile sweetly at their colleagues, but inside are consumed with jealousy. They play the part of the pure virgin, but their minds are filled with lustful images and fantasies. They seem content with their lot in life, but cry inside with greed. They gossip under the guise of sharing information. They lie but rationalize that it's just a slight exaggeration.

The longer we are disciples, the easier it is to come to all the church services, give financially, say the right things and give all the right impressions. Women can learn pretty quickly how to paint the portrait of a life that is above question. We can seem to be "fine Christian women" but harbor in our hearts a hypocrisy that is known only to God. We can be friendly and warm to everyone, but in reality carry a resentment that has never been confessed. We can be married and upstanding and outwardly moral, but secretly fantasize about other men. We can talk to Christians about hurting for the lost and the need to bring them the gospel, yet be cowardly and silent when around our non-Christian friends. These are all examples of hiding our "bad" behind a facade of "good." This is insincerity. Jacob's insincerity began over a bowl of stew and erupted into treachery. The same can happen to any of us if we are not determined to hold on to our integrity and maintain soft hearts before God and others.

The Miserable Masquerade

> *Jacob went close to his father Isaac, who touched him and said, "The voice is the voice of Jacob, but the hands are the hands of Esau." He did not recognize him, for his hands were hairy like those of his brother Esau; so he blessed him. "Are you really my son Esau?" he asked.*
>
> *"I am," he replied (Genesis 27:22-24).*

When the time had come for Isaac to bless his son, a scheme unfolded that would bring about the ultimate break in Jacob and Esau's relationship. Goaded by his mother, Jacob agreed to deceive his father by dressing up like Esau to receive the blessing. Although Rebekah was the instigator of this deception, Jacob fully understood the trickery to which he was consenting and made the personal decision to manipulate and lie. When Isaac expressed surprise that "Esau" had returned so quickly, Jacob quickly covered his tracks with the excuse: "God granted me success." (How many other times in history has God been used as a scapegoat for people's sins?) When his father became suspicious, Jacob quickly assured him that he was, indeed, the older son—deeper and deeper layers of lying. Isaac in turn, gave Jacob the prophetic blessing that was meant for Esau.

This type of masquerade is not restricted to dressing up in disguises. Haven't we all pretended to be something we're not? Haven't we put on an act to get something we want? Maybe what we wanted was recognition or praise or respect or simply to be accepted. But deep down, we were miserable, because we knew we were not being real.

I learned early on about putting on a facade. As a teenager, I became interested in the theater, but my acting abilities were stronger in real life than on the stage. Depending on the "audience," I could be sweet, innocent and respectable, or I could be downright obscene. The two-faced person I became certainly succeeded in getting things I wanted, but I lived in fear that people might see the real me. Getting to know Jesus was the only solution to my problem. It's an amazing thing: The more I know him, the more I know myself, and the more I can be myself with others.

Disciples must be able to say, "What you see is what you get." Pretending that all is right in our lives while harboring sin will not cut it. Even worse is the pretense that we commit more times than we want to admit: going along with the crowd—knowing we should speak up for what we believe, knowing we should be real about our convictions, but cowering and becoming "one of them" in order to be accepted. The consequences of these kinds of disguises can ruin our lives.

Facades are uncomfortable as well as unrealistic. Because Jacob resorted to dishonest means to promote himself, the result was a family torn apart, and Jacob was forced to flee for his life.

The Dream

> When he reached a certain place, he stopped for the night because the sun had set. Taking one of the stones there, he put it under his head and lay down to sleep. He had a dream in which he saw a stairway resting on the earth, with its top reaching to heaven, and the angels of God were ascending and descending on it (Genesis 28:11-12).

Escaping the clutches of a domineering mother and a vengeful brother, Jacob began a new chapter in his life. Up to this point, "God" was the God of his father, Isaac. (See Genesis 27:20 where Jacob speaks of him as "the Lord your God.") The blessings that were to be his came through promises made to his parents or through his parents, and not to him personally. As far as we know, Jacob had never had his own personal encounter with God.

All that changed at a "certain place" on the way to Haran. It was one of those places, one of those times that he would remember forever. As he rested for the evening, God revealed himself to Jacob in a dream. Angels descending and ascending on a stairway from heaven to the earth were the background for the promise from God:

> There above it stood the LORD, and he said: "I am the LORD, the God of your father Abraham and the God of

Isaac. I will give you and your descendants the land on which you are lying. Your descendants will be like the dust of the earth, and you will spread out to the west and to the east, to the north and to the south. All peoples on earth will be blessed through you and your offspring. I am with you and will watch over you wherever you go, and I will bring you back to this land. I will not leave you until I have done what I have promised you"
(Genesis 28:13-15).

Jacob's response when he awoke was to make a vow to God and erect a pillar in remembrance of the great event. Many years later, he would return to this place and reaffirm his faithfulness to his God (Genesis 35). Most likely this place was not a spectacularly beautiful spot, nor one where anyone might expect an encounter with God. But for Jacob it was a point of turning, a place of radical change.

Hopefully, we all have "certain places" that we can revisit, either in person or in thought. Those certain places in our lives are places where significant events occurred, or where life-changing decisions were made: the place where you were baptized, or where you met your best friend, or where your husband proposed, or where you decided that a certain character sin would no longer dominate your life. I love to visit the house in which the Scriptures finally began to make sense to me. I can stand in a certain room and recall catching a glimpse, for the first time, of the incredible love of God. The four walls in that room are not particularly special or different, but to me they are precious because they remind me of a great event in my life.

We've heard about the importance of "making memories" with our families: going places and doing things that we will remember with fondness and affection. There is an equal need for us to make memories with our God. Finding certain places that are important to our relationship with God builds our intimacy with him.

If you were to drive with me through the Boston area, where I have lived for the last several years, I could show you special spots that have become significant to me over time. There's the school playground where I spent a wintry Sunday afternoon crying over some hurts and failures, and was reminded of the tenderness and comfort of God. There's a restaurant where I had a long and challenging talk with a friend. (I think we ate there, too, but I can't remember that!) There's the cemetery that I bicycled to one sunny day and, as I wandered among the tombstones, resolved to make specific changes in my life. The memory of what happened at those "certain places" encourages me and revitalizes my faith, even after a long time.

Jacob was just beginning a journey that would both challenge and inspire him, but the memory of his "certain place" would remain in his heart and in his mind. It wasn't enough that his father and his grandfather had encounters with God; he had to have his own introduction to the Lord. In the midst of the struggles that he would face in the years to come, he would ponder the promise God had given him—the promise that he would one day return to this place and that his descendants would bless the earth. He would always recall the night he rested his head on a stone and dreamt of angels. He would remember, and in remembering, he would know that *his* God would never leave him.

What Goes Around Comes Around

> *When morning came, there was Leah! So Jacob said to Laban, "What is this you have done to me? I served you for Rachel, didn't I? Why have you deceived me?" (Genesis 29:25).*

Having an encounter with God certainly does not mean that everything is smooth sailing from then on. For Jacob, much of his trouble in life was just beginning. When he became a married man, God used several circumstances and several people to teach him the character lessons he needed to learn.

Upon his arrival in Haran, Jacob immediately hooked up with family members, specifically his mother's older brother, Laban. His delight in finding relatives was intensified when he laid eyes on Laban's daughter, the lovely Rachel. Now, if this were a movie or a television show, Jacob and Rachel would have tied the knot within the next sixty minutes. But this was real life, and Jacob was willing to work for Laban seven years to have Rachel's hand in marriage. Seven years! And here come some of the most romantic words found in Scripture: "But they seemed like only a few days to him because of his love for her" (Genesis 29:20).

There is a glitch in this love story, however. When the sun rose after the consummation of the marriage, Jacob realized he had wed Leah, Rachel's older sister. As shocked and dismayed as Jacob must have been to realize that he had been deceived by Laban, there surely was a flashback in his mind replaying a similar trick. Jacob had been blinded by darkness and veils; Isaac, his father, had been blinded by his own eyes and by Jacob's disguise. In the darkness, Leah had felt the same as Rachel; to Isaac, Jacob had felt the same as his older brother. Jacob had no cause to distrust Laban's agreement; Isaac had no reason to suspect that Jacob would impersonate his brother. Jacob had been led to believe he was with the younger sister; Isaac had been led to believe he was with the older brother. The treachery he had committed now came back to haunt him.

"What goes around comes around," or "The Laban Principle," as some have called it, is exhibited by this incident. Jacob deceived, then he was deceived. We might call this poetic justice for Jacob...but what if it happens to us? The concept is true: How we treat others is how we eventually will be treated ourselves. God will never let us get past a sin without helping us to see the pain it causes. He can and will forgive us, but he will make sure we learn the lesson. He will put us in situations where we can see ourselves in others, and he will use whomever he wants to show us what we must learn. The Scripture tells us clearly, "For in the same way you judge others, you will be judged, and with the measure you use, it will be measured to you (Matthew 7:2).

When my children were little, they were the classic examples of the term, "fussy eaters." I would beg, plead and coax them, "Eat! Eat!" remembering all the while how my parents had anguished over my own diminutive appetite. I tried, "Here comes the airplane" with a spoon filled with yummy pureed carrots flying around their excited little faces—to no avail. As soon as the "airplane" came in for a landing, the "airport" closed down, leaving the carrots to crash-land on the bib, on the kids and on me! "The Laban Principle," I would mutter to myself, knowing that I was now experiencing the anxiety I had caused my parents. While my problem with the kids' eating habits was not devastating, other examples of the principle can be very telling. Here are some suggestions of situations where the Laban Principle might be taking effect:

- You're sick and in the hospital and your visitors and cards of encouragement are few. But when was the last time *you* visited the sick? Did *you* forget or neglect to send cards when you knew of a friend or neighbor who was hospitalized? Your loneliness and discouragement are, hopefully, teaching you to be more sensitive to others who are ill.
- A friend is trying to help you to be more like Jesus, but has said some things that hurt your feelings and

has misunderstood some of your intentions. You could get a resentful attitude toward her, or you *could* bring to mind that time *you* spoke harshly with the person you were trying to help. You could consider that you have misjudged people at times. Instead of becoming bitter, focusing on the hurt and defending yourself, you could appreciate her efforts and hear the heart of your friend's concern for you. She might be absolutely right!

- You are the subject of some gossip: Someone has betrayed a confidence, or has misconstrued some information about you. Haven't *you* at some time opened your mouth one time too many and said some things you regretted? Don't you understand now how hurtful gossip can be, and will you resolve never to be party to it again?

- Your kids are being disrespectful and are not obeying you. They roll their eyes and talk back at you. Do you see *yourself* in their faces? Are they merely imitating how *you* speak to your husband? Do they imitate your example of unsubmissiveness? Do you realize that you must show them how to be respectful by being so with their father?

None of the examples above are given as excuses to accept sinful, unkind behavior, but to aid us in looking at situations from a different perspective. What can we learn from the Laban Principle? We can learn to forgive. We can stop being complaining, whining victims who never get treated right and become gracious and compassionate human beings who understand our own human frailties, as well as the frailties of others. We can be merciful, as we have been shown mercy. Above all, we can be grateful that God has shown us where we each need to change.

Hopefully, when Jacob felt the sting of betrayal, he began to understand the devastation he had caused his brother, Esau, and his father, Isaac. Throughout his lifetime, Jacob would learn time and again the hurt that is caused by deceit. He would suffer from the trickery of Laban, his wives and his sons. Throughout Jacob's tumultuous life, he would continue to be purified by God.

Torn Between Two Lovers

> *When Rachel saw that she was not bearing Jacob any children, she became jealous of her sister. So she said to Jacob, "Give me children, or I'll die!" (Genesis 30:1).*

The account of Rachel and Leah is enough to talk anyone out of polygamy! In fact, God later supplied a command forbidding two living sisters from marrying the same man (Leviticus 18:18). The jealousy and competition between these two women was intensified in their race to see who could have the most children. Rachel was Jacob's favorite, but she was barren. (However, Rachel in time gave birth to two sons.) Leah was homely and unloved, but was quite fertile. It's sad to think that these two women, who at one time had probably been great friends, sharing dreams and clothes and giggles, now became the most bitter of enemies.

Through the years, with the contributions of Rachel and Leah's maids, Bilhah and Zilpah, Jacob had twelve sons and one daughter. With the birth of each child, the contest intensified, with the sisters even naming their sons according to their attitudes. Adding to the conflict was the continual mistrust between Jacob and Laban. In fact, the only time we see Rachel and Leah being of one mind was in their agreement to run away from Laban and return with Jacob to his homeland.

Just as Jacob and his entourage were escaping, Laban discovered their absence and chased them down, especially enraged by the fact that his household "gods" had been stolen. Unbeknownst to Jacob, Rachel had taken them. When Laban searched the camp, he could not find them because Rachel had hidden them in her saddle. When she did not rise to greet her father, she used the excuse that has been used for centuries: "I'm having my period" (Genesis 31:35).

Perhaps Rachel was getting even with her father for all that he had done. Perhaps she really trusted in the idols or they represented financial security. Whatever the case, Rachel found a way out of a difficult spot by blaming it on her period. If you were starting to daydream, wondering what sibling rivalry and polygamy and idols had to do with you, I'm sure this statement woke you up! Rachel was a woman just like you and me, a woman who had hormonal ups and downs, and a woman who covered up her sin with her menstrual cycle. Lest you start rationalizing that you've never sat on household idols, let's think of other ways that "that time of the month" has been used:

- "I know I lost my temper; it's that time of the month."
- "I can't help crying; it's that time of the month."
- "I'm a bit spacy; it's that time of the month."

Or, in a more bizarre but true example:

- "I killed my husband; it's that time of the month!"

While it is one thing to recognize our physical limitations, it's another to accept sinful behavior based on a hormonal surge. Lately, the excuse has extended to premenstrual syndrome as well as postmenstrual syndrome. In other words, no matter what time of the month it is, we have an excuse to be weak, emotional, lazy or completely out of control!

It is helpful to understand that the feelings we have may be caused by our periods or by the onset of menopause, but it is useless, based on that, to tolerate sin. I know that my hormones can cause me to be anxious and irritable. But I can also get anxious and irritable on hot days, or cold days, or when I'm dealing with an unpleasant person, or for scores of other reasons! Do any of these things allow me to accept sin? No. I have to recognize the temptations and adjust my temperament accordingly. I must also be responsible enough to know my body's need for rest and a healthy diet, which can help to balance out my emotions. Our feelings can be controlled by the power of God, who understands women better than we understand ourselves.

Rachel got away with her sin, but she risked her life. Jacob had pronounced a death sentence on the thief, not knowing it was she. Because of her theft, Rachel intensified the animosity between her husband and her father—an animosity that was soothed only by a covenant before God between the two men.

Wrestling with God

> *When the messengers returned to Jacob, they said, "We went to your brother Esau, and now he is coming to meet you, and four hundred men are with him" (Genesis 32:6).*

Jacob was finally in a situation that he knew he could not handle. After twenty years of being away, he was still terrified of Esau. Perhaps the trials that Jacob had been through made him even more aware of the hatred his brother might be feeling. He had no assurance that Esau had come in peace and, in fact, assumed that he came to kill him and his family—after all, Esau was the skilled hunter of the two. All of this drove Jacob to his knees.

> "...O God of my father Abraham, God of my father Isaac, O LORD who said to me, 'Go back to your country and your relatives, and I will make you prosper.' I am unworthy of all the kindness and faithfulness you have shown your servant. I had only my staff when I crossed this Jordan, but now I have become two groups. Save me, I pray, from the hand of my brother Esau, for I am afraid he will come and attack me, and also the mothers with their children. But you have said, 'I will surely make you prosper and will make your descendants like the sand of the sea, which cannot be counted'" (Genesis 32:9-12).

In the line-up of characters in the book of Genesis, Jacob has not been the most lovable guy. He paid dearly for his craftiness and deceit, but it's still difficult to have a lot of sympathy for him—up until this point. Seeing this man humbly begging God to save him and his family shows me the side of him I'd been looking for all along. Now I see a man who recognizes that all he has is from God. I see a man who knows he needs help. I see a man who is clinging to the promises of God.

Even after that heartfelt prayer, Jacob recognized his need to be alone and continue to draw near to God. "Wrestling with God" is a term we often use to describe our prayer life, but Jacob meant it literally. All night long he wrestled and would not let go until he was blessed. When the sun rose, Jacob had a new name (*Israel*), a sore hip and the confidence to face whatever the day would hold (Genesis 32:24-32).

You are probably not facing a vengeful brother coming with four hundred men, but if you are a disciple, you are constantly facing things that are just plain frightening. I might add that if you are *not* facing things that scare you, then you are *not* following Jesus! Christianity is not a trip into the comfort zone, but an adventure in faith. Each day we should be facing new challenges which push us and demand that we go further than the day before.

The biggest challenge we all face is the challenge to share our faith. God has called us to reach out to others and tell them the gospel of Jesus Christ. Sometimes it feels as if facing an unbeliever is as terrifying as facing an army of four hundred men. Sometimes we don't know what to expect: Will we be sharing with a person who has an open and tender heart toward the word of God, or will we be going toe-to-toe with a hostile adversary? The fear can only drive us to our knees. Unlike Jacob, this is not a once-in-a-lifetime challenge, but a challenge we face every single day. Every day we must be committed to facing the lost and offering them hope.

Whatever other challenges we may face, we can't face them without prayer. For every disciple, there are times of wrestling through doubts and fears. There are times we can't stop praying until we feel confident of God's presence. It may take an hour, or it may take all night, but we must wrestle until we *know* that God will bless us.

Randy, my husband, had suffered with Hodgkin's Disease (cancer of the lymph node system) when he was a teenager. While we were engaged to be married, he became very ill with some mysterious symptoms. The doctors were not certain of the cause of his problems, and sent him to a hospital in another city for evaluation. When he left town, I was devastated. I was so afraid of a recurrence of the cancer; so afraid that he might die and that I would lose the love of my life.

Before I had the chance to completely fall apart, a friend took me aside, looked me squarely in the eye and said, "Kay, are you going to allow this to be a time of victory or a time of defeat?" The talk jolted me. I expected a shoulder to cry on and soft words of sympathy, and here she was giving me a rock-hard challenge! Later that day, I found a private place and spent hours in prayer. I wrestled with God, and finally let go of Randy. I remembered that he belonged to God, not to me, and that God was in control of his cancer. I decided that no matter what happened, I would spend the following days in God's strength and comfort.

As it turned out, Randy's illness had been caused by an infection of one of the wires in his sternum. (The sternum had to be cut for surgery years before, and the wires held the sternum together until it could fully heal.) He was placed on antibiotics and was back to good health within a week. Imagine if I had spent those days fretful and wringing my hands with anxiety. That would have been the natural thing for me to do, but because I wrestled in prayer and gave up my fears to God, I am able to look back on that time and know that it was a victory.

Reunion

He himself went on ahead and bowed down to the ground seven times as he approached his brother.

But Esau ran to meet Jacob and embraced him; he threw his arms around his neck and kissed him. And they wept" (Genesis 33:3-4).

After all the fears and all the years, Esau and Jacob were finally reunited. Both men had been prospered so much by the hand of God that neither felt cheated. Esau's warm affection toward his brother is particularly poignant considering his previous plans to kill Jacob. His forgiveness and love brought about the closure of a deeply hurtful episode in their lives.

When Jesus told the parable of the Prodigal Son (Luke 15), I wonder if he had this reunion in mind. The estrangement between the father and the son ended when the son finally returned home, not certain what his father's response would be, and was greeted with hugs and tears and celebration. The message seems to be that our relationship with God can never be based on our bargaining or manipulation, nor does he want us to stay away because of our fear. God just wants a relationship with us.

Jacob, or Israel, had to struggle to get his relationship with God. As the years went on, Jacob faced other struggles in his life: the death of Rachel, the rape of his only daughter, the loss of his beloved son, Joseph. The lesson we learn from Jacob is not that he did everything right or lived a charmed life, but that he struggled and overcame. He was a wrestler, determined to receive the blessings of God. Life wasn't easy for him, yet he pushed through. Isn't that what we all must do? Don't we all have struggles that we must wrestle through? Don't we all have to cling to the promises of God? This is what Jacob learned to do. He learned that what really mattered was having a relationship with God. The wrestling lasted only one night, but Jacob never again let go of God.

· *Taking It Home* ·

1. Jacob and Esau were born on the same day, members of the same family, but they were very different from each other. Think of someone, either a natural or a spiritual brother or sister, from whom you are very different. In what ways has it been difficult to understand the other person? To feel love for him or her? What causes you to get irritated? How have you been able to learn to appreciate and love him or her?

2. Do your sins tend to be the type that are obvious or the type that trail behind you? Have you been around the church long enough to have "learned the ropes"? Do you act one way on the outside while feeling and thinking a different way on the inside? How can you go after this tendency in your character? How eager are you to repent and change?

3. Finish this sentence: The reason I tend to wear masks is because...

4. How can you help those in your life to be more real?

5. Think of some places that hold special meaning in your memory. What are some things that happened at those places that made a positive impact on you? How does it affect you when you visit that place in person or in your mind?

6. When was the last time you spent the night in prayer? When was the last time you wrestled through your doubts or your fears and would not leave God until you were confident? When was the last time you devoted a weekend or even a day to prayer and study of the Word?

The Wait

8

Genesis
37-47

CASE HISTORY OF: *Joseph*

AGE: *17*

MARITAL STATUS: *Single*

BACKGROUND: *Joseph is a good-looking, pleasant young male who has experienced continual sibling conflict. He comes from a dysfunctional family. He grew up with his mother and his step-mother, as well as numerous stepbrothers, one stepsister and one full brother. He witnessed much discord between the two mothers. His father had other mistresses as well. He also was witness to a potential war between his father and his uncle. His sister was raped when she was a very young woman, and her brothers were part of a vengeful act of violence against the rapist and his family. Many were killed in this "gang war," and although Joseph was too young to be a part of it, he felt the effects in the family. His mother died in childbirth delivering his younger brother. His oldest brother has been involved in an incestuous-type affair with his father's mistress. This is known among the family members, but has not been discussed. His grandfather recently passed away. Joseph is suffering from delusions of greatness; he is having recurring dreams about crops and planets bowing down to him.*

DIAGNOSIS: *My opinion is that Joseph is permanently scarred due to his extremely troubled family history. As he faces adulthood, the possibility that he will resort to violence in some shape or form is inevitable. He is a victim, one who in all probability will bring trouble to himself and to his family. Surprisingly, Joseph seems unaffected by his traumatic upbringing, but that is probably due to the repression of his emotions. His confident and cheerful outlook are most likely the result of the controlling influence of his brothers and father. Unfortunately, Joseph's case shows the difficulties that are typical of families today.*

SIGNED: Ms. E.X. Pert

If social workers existed during Joseph's lifetime, the above synopsis of him is what would probably have been written. As you will see, the "expert" prognosis proved to be false and Joseph will be seen to rise above the negative influences of his past. The story of Joseph is at the same time heart-breaking and heart-moving; more than anything, it is a story assuring us that we don't have to be victims, but can become victors! It is increasingly popular in our time to blame others for how we have turned out. Blaming our parents, our siblings, our teachers, our church or our society makes it a simple thing to avoid all responsibility for our sin. A woman named Anna Russell wrote a poem that humorously points out the foibles in this type of thinking:[1]

> I went to my psychiatrist to be psychoanalyzed.
> To find out why I killed the cat and blacked my husband's eyes.
> He laid me on a downy couch to see what he could find,
> And here is what he dredged up from my subconscious mind:
> When I was one, my mommie hid my dolly in a trunk,
> And so it follows naturally that I am always drunk.

[1]Jay Adams. *Competent to Counsel* (Grand Rapids, Michigan: Zondervan, 1970), 8.

When I was two, I saw my father kiss the maid one day,
And that is why I suffer now from kleptomania.
At three I had the feeling of ambivalence toward my
    brothers,
And so it follows naturally I poison all my lovers.
But I am happy; now I've learned the lesson this has taught;
That everything I do that's wrong is someone else's fault.

This is not to say that traumatic experiences are something to be laughed at. Divorce, abuse and incest are only a few of the issues that plague millions of children today, causing them to grow up into insecure and unhappy adults. The good news is that God can give us the power to overcome any background.

Years ago I heard the story of a young girl who had been assaulted by a stranger in a relatively safe area, taken to an obscure spot and violently raped. As she was rushed to the hospital, the police were able to locate the girl's mother so that she could meet her daughter there. When the mother found her daughter in the hospital bed, covered with bruises, she rushed to her side and embraced her. With tears flowing down her cheeks, the first thing she said to her daughter was, "Hating this man is not an option." The two women wrestled through the agony of that violent act, but resolved that it would not destroy their commitment to love and forgiveness. As much as it must have pained the mother to see her daughter's innocence stolen away, it would have pained her more to see her daughter become bitter, blaming all men for the crime committed by one man. Her gentleness and her strength helped the girl to recover quickly. She will certainly never forget that horrible night, but she was equipped by her mother with the strength to overcome it.

Joseph is the classic example of a man who, in spite of insurmountable odds, kept his trust in a loving and powerful

God and continued to do what was right. He was equipped by God to maintain his righteousness and his faith. He may have started his life with many strikes against him, but we can be encouraged to see how God used those hardships to bring about his purpose.

The Dream

> When he told his father as well as his brothers [about his dream], his father rebuked him and said, "What is this dream you had? Will your mother and I and your brothers actually come and bow down to the ground before you?" His brothers were jealous of him, but his father kept the matter in mind (Genesis 37:10-11).

Following the older boys around like a puppy dog, Joseph was probably regarded as a pesky nuisance. He was "Daddy's pet," just a kid to ignore, a typical little brother. Then he had the audacity to share with them those outrageous dreams—sheaves of grain and stars in the sky, clearly representing the older brothers, bowing down to him! "Who does he think he is?" they may have protested. "I changed that kid's diapers and wiped his nose. Does he think I'll ever bow down to him?" Joseph's father, definitely not pleased that he had revealed the dream and pridefully chafing at its implications for him, couldn't help but consider the possibilities, remembering that he too had been strongly influenced by a dream (Genesis 28:10-17). As the Scripture describes, "His brothers were jealous of him, but his father kept the matter in mind" (Genesis 37:11).

Should Joseph have told everyone about the dream? Should he have simply kept it to himself? Was it a boastful attitude that compelled him to talk about it? Or was he just innocently making conversation without discerning how it might make the others feel? Whatever his intentions were, Joseph's statements exposed the jealousy and pride of his older brothers. As the older men in the family, they were not about to have this young whipper-snapper think that he was better than they! Their superiority had to be asserted. The older would never bow down to the younger.

Learning from Anyone

One of the greatest blessings of the church is the relationships we share with one another—relationships that train us and help us to grow spiritually. (By the way, these types of friendships are not an option. God's plan is quite clear: We must be taught and challenged by others, and we must allow others into our lives. The woman who is independent and resists discipleship is the woman who is not obeying God.) The ideal "discipling" relationship is one that involves an older woman training a younger woman (Titus 2:4). Through these partnerships we can watch and learn from the example of one who is more mature. The danger we may face, however, is in forgetting how much we can learn from those who are younger than we are. As we grow older, we can smile condescendingly at the young, considering ourselves so much wiser that we harden our hearts to all they can teach us.

My husband and I were newlyweds and fresh out of college when we went into the full-time ministry. Full of high hopes and dreams, we set out to fill the earth with the love of Christ. Our first stop was in a small, dying church in South Carolina. Most of the members of that congregation were old enough to be my grandmother. They admired our zeal and enthusiasm and promised they would wholeheartedly support our mission to save lost souls in that city.

What we didn't know until a few months later was that their "support" meant patting us on our backs and telling us to get out there and do it, but leave them out of it! Randy and I, in our naiveté, tried our hardest to get them to join us in the mission. The typical responses we received were crushing: "Who do you think you are? Do you think you can come in here and tell us how to be Christians? Don't you know we're older than you? You can't tell us what to do with our lives!" Others attempted to let us down easier: "When you get a little older, you'll understand. You haven't had children; you haven't been married as long as I have. You can't possibly understand my situation." The message was loud and clear: Unless you are as old as I am, or have done what I've done, or have experienced what I've experienced, then butt out!

This is not to say that I did a perfect job in approaching those who were older. I have no doubt that there were times when I wasn't as respectful as I should have been, or was arrogant in my communication. But I also knew that what I was saying was truth—it wasn't my opinion or my idea, but it was from the lips of Jesus Christ. I vowed at that time that I would never close my heart or my ears to hear what a younger person had to tell me. I have striven through the years to have a "learner's spirit" with young and old alike. Whether it's my children or the youngest Christian, if someone can show me how to be a better follower of Jesus, then I want to listen!

Betrayal

> *Now Joseph had been taken down to Egypt. Potiphar, an Egyptian who was one of Pharaoh's officials, the captain of the guard, bought him from the Ishmaelites who had taken him there (Genesis 39:1).*

The hatred and jealousy of Joseph's brothers was so intense that they sold him into slavery; then they covered up the deed by leading their father to believe he was killed by a wild animal. We can only wonder what went through young Joseph's mind as he experienced this unbelievable betrayal. He must have thought, *They're just trying to scare me. They'll come back soon and get me out of here.* How relieved he must have felt when they dropped the rope to pull him out...only to have his heart sink again as he realized his own brothers were about to sell him as a slave. Bound and led away by the merchants, he pleaded with his brothers to save him, but his cries fell on deaf ears (Genesis 42:21).

Traveling across hundreds of miles of unfamiliar terrain into completely unknown territory, he had plenty of time to decide how he should feel about the strange turn of events in his life. Maybe he asked himself if God could make his dream come true in a foreign land. Perhaps he wrestled with feelings of hatred toward his brothers, or looked longingly into the welcoming pool of self-pity. Maybe he considered that life was now only a question of survival. At some point on that journey, Joseph must have made a decision to make the best of a bad situation. Convinced that God could work anywhere and everywhere, he must have made the choice that he would not hate his brothers; that he would adapt to his new home and use all his abilities and talents fully, trusting that God would come through with his part of the bargain. No moaning, no groaning—only a deep conviction that he could walk into a new culture, a new language and a new life with God as his only companion.

Joseph's resolve paid off. His work for his new master was so successful that he was entrusted with everything in the household. Potiphar had complete confidence in his young slave and could attend to his duties without a single concern. Joseph's diligence at his work is a great example to any woman in the working world. He was honest, reliable, respectful: He was a blessing to Potiphar (Genesis 39:5). In the same way, our presence at our places of employment should be a blessing to the employer. He or she should be able to have complete confidence in us because they are assured of our integrity. I have heard of bosses who have been so impressed with Christians in their office that they have asked specifically if others from the church could work there as well! Would your boss want to hire others just like you?

Speaking of the workplace, there is a term that is widely used to describe an unfortunate situation that often arises when men and women work together: "sexual harassment." To find a whopper of a sample of sexual harassment, one only has to look at what happened to Joseph. Work for Potiphar was going well until Potiphar's wife noticed Joseph. This young slave was the epitome of the perfect man: He was "well-built and handsome"; he was hard-working, and he was dependable. Potiphar's wife watched him, liked what she saw, and propositioned him: "Come to bed with me," she said (Genesis 39:7). Could she have been any less discreet?

Keep in mind that Joseph was being tempted at a time in his life when his sexual desires were incredibly strong. Here was a woman who was dying to go to bed with him—what an ego-booster to any young man—and the set-up was perfect. No one would find out. The temptation was constant and direct. Day after day she badgered him, and day after day he refused her.

Sexual temptations surround us constantly, and none of us is immune to their pull. Joseph's reaction to temptation is the same reaction we must have: He ran away! (Genesis 39:12). He never even toyed with the idea. He knew that even if no one else ever found out about his indiscretion, God would. He knew that to give in to Potiphar's wife would be a sin against God (Genesis 39:9). He hoped that by resisting her, she would finally leave him alone. But when she did not, his only recourse was to flee.

In 2 Timothy 2:22 Paul instructs us to "flee the evil desires of youth," and he adds in Ephesians 5:3, "among you there must not even be a hint of sexual immorality." While the world encourages us to indulge, God commands us to abstain from any sexual activity that is not a part of the marriage relationship. God created the whole concept of sexual enjoyment, but he knew that sex could never be what he wanted it to be outside the bounds of marriage.

What do you do when you are sexually tempted? Do you linger with the fellow who's luring you? Do you ponder over that thought for a while? Do you watch a little longer, read a little further, listen a little harder? Do you allow yourself to get into dangerous situations—like a parked car late at night, or alone with a boyfriend in his room or home? People who say that they "fell into sin" are fooling only themselves. Getting into a private place and removing clothes is a lot more complicated than "falling." There are too many women who exchange a few moments of pleasure for the confidence that comes from not sinning against God. Joseph fled from sin, and if he can do it, so can we!

If you do the right thing, God will bless you, right? Well, yes, but it may not be in the way we would expect. Joseph did the right thing in running away from Potiphar's wife, but the reward he received was an accusation of rape and a trip to prison. Maybe now Joseph will give up on being the "good guy." Maybe now he'll give up on God. Read on.

Seize the Day

Even in prison, Joseph knew that the Lord was with him. God "showed him kindness and granted him favor in the eyes of the prison warden" (Genesis 39:21). Obviously, while Joseph was there he did not simply pine away the days wishing he were somewhere else. He used the time he had productively, and because of that, the time for his release was hastened. Interpreting dreams for servants of the king gave him a notoriety that would have been lost had he simply wallowed in depression, stayed to himself and considered the jail sentence to be a waste of time. Even when one of the servants forgot all about him, Joseph did not become a bitter victim. When Pharoah had a dream that needed interpretation, he seized the opportunity to give glory to God (Genesis 41:16).

Unfortunately, I know that in various times in my life I have been tempted to waste time by wishing I were somewhere else. Our residence in Munich, Germany, as missionaries was originally going to be limited to two to three weeks, at which time we were to move on to Paris, France. That was my plan. That was my husband's plan. But that was not God's plan. Due to a delay in receiving our visas, we remained in Germany for several months. My husband seized the situation with gusto, using the opportunity to strengthen the Christians there and to study the Bible with more Germans. He did an incredible job making sure that the church had a solid foundation. I, too set out to minister to Christians and non-Christians alike, but not with the same gusto as my husband. I loved Germany and loved the people there. I went about my work diligently, but inside there were times that I was incredibly discontent. It was autumn, and I couldn't enroll my children in school because we didn't know how long we would stay. We didn't have an apartment, and had to spend the majority of the time hopping from one hotel room to another until we could find a more suitable place to live. Added to that was the "unknown"—how long would this last? During a time when I could have been thoroughly enjoying life on the mission field, I found myself worrying way too much about how long it would take before we got back to our original plan.

In early December of that year, I decided to really put my heart into where I was. I decided to stop being anxious about the future. I put a plan into action to meet the kids' need for schooling. I started working harder to speak the German language. I decided that since I was there, it was time to give it my all and not just part of my all. As is typical when God knows he has our hearts, within the next two weeks of that decision, we received our visas to go to France.

Today, years later, I'm so grateful that I was able to be in Germany. Even in the midst of my discontentment, we were able to see many become Christians. I have such fond memories of the people who were there, and I am so proud of what the church there has become. I only wish that I had "seized the day" sooner, as my husband did. Thanks to him and God (and in spite of myself), our time in Germany was a blessing to my life.

Worth the Wait

> Then Pharaoh said to Joseph, "Since God has made all this known to you, there is no one so discerning and wise as you. You shall be in charge of my palace, and all my people are to submit to your orders. Only with respect to the throne will I be greater than you."
>
> So Pharaoh said to Joseph, "I hereby put you in charge of the whole land of Egypt" (Genesis 41:39-41).

Because of Joseph's success in interpreting Pharaoh's dream, he was given a position of honor in the greatest civilization of that era. His expert ability in administration was instrumental in preventing a catastrophic famine from wiping out the nation. Even the surrounding nations had suffered because of the scarcity of food. While we might view the famine as a tragic situation, God used it to bring about the reunion of Joseph with his family and the fulfillment of the promise he had given to them long ago.

When Joseph's brothers came to Egypt to buy grain, they approached Joseph, not recognizing him, bowing their faces to the ground. But Joseph recognized them, and remembered his dreams from long before (Genesis 42:9). After several escapades, Joseph finally revealed himself to his brothers, and the family was together once more. There are so many heart-warming scenes throughout these circumstances: Joseph turning aside to weep when he saw the anxiety of his brothers, and again when he saw his youngest brother, Benjamin (Genesis 42:24; 43:30); Judah, willing to remain as a prisoner instead of Benjamin, out of fear that his father would die if Benjamin did not return (Genesis 44:30-31); the reunion of Joseph with his father, Israel (Genesis 46:29). These were real people with real emotions, and God allows us an intimate glimpse of them through his Word.

Joseph had to wait many years to see his dreams come true. He had to wait a long time for success, for love, for resolution. He waited, but while he waited, he was used by God. His wasn't the life he had planned; it wasn't the one he would have chosen for himself. But it was the one life God had given him, and he used it well. While he waited, God worked on his heart and the hearts of others so that the most good could be done. Even though we often consider waiting a necessary evil, God considers it a necessary good.

Are you waiting for your dreams to come true? Are you waiting for God to bless you? Then wait patiently and joyfully, but use the waiting time well. Don't waste your days wishing you were in another place or in another time. When we're young, it's so easy to waste our lives wishing we were older: "When I'm out of school, I can...." "When I'm married, I'll be able to...." "When I have kids, then I'll...." "When the kids are grown, I can...." Then when we get older, we waste our lives wishing for the past, longing for the "good old days." There is a scripture that addresses this kind of thinking: "Do not say, 'Why were the old days better than these?' For it is not wise to ask such questions" (Ecclesiastes 7:10). The lesson again is to use the here and now, to "seize the day." As the Psalmist says, "This is the day the Lord has made; let us rejoice and be glad in it" (Psalm 118:24).

The Right Perspective

> *"And now, do not be distressed and do not be angry*
> *with yourselves for selling me here, because it was to*
> *save lives that God sent me ahead of you....But God*
> *sent me ahead of you to preserve for you a remnant on*
> *earth and to save your lives by a great deliverance"*
> *(Genesis 45:5,7, emphasis added).*

"But God." These are the two words that make all the difference in the world. They are the words that reveal the heart and mind of Joseph. He knew the hardships he had faced, and he recognized the bad thing his brothers had done by selling him. But he also knew God, and he could see God's hand working in his life.

"But God" are the words that change our perspective on life. It is the attitude that enables us to see all things, both good and bad, and know that God can use them to bring about his purposes: "And we know that in all things God works for the good of those who love him, who have been called according to his purpose" (Romans 8:28). This scripture is not a panacea to say reluctantly: "Oh well, I guess it will all work out in the end," but rather, it describes the deep conviction of those who are called by God.

"But God" is the reason that apartheid was overturned about the same time Christians arrived in South Africa to plant a church there. "But God" is the reason that Communism fell just when disciples showed up in Russia. "But God" is the reason the Berlin Wall was demolished as the Berlin mission team was being formed. In the swirling and tumultuous political arena, God is always working so that more people can become disciples!

It is imperative for disciples to have the perspective of trusting in God's ways and God's plans despite the circumstances at hand. When Peter objected to Jesus' explanation of his suffering and crucifixion, Jesus' response was severe: "Get behind me, Satan! You are a stumbling block to me; you do not have in mind the things of God, but the things of men" (Matthew 16:23). Peter had been looking at things from his own humanistic, worldly point of view, and not from God's point of view. That perspective was dangerous to the cause of Christ.

Our outlook on life's circumstances must be: "What will help the most people to be saved?" God will use catastrophes, political upheavals, tragedies and victories if they will provide an opportunity for people to hear the gospel. In Joseph's case, God used jealous brothers, a lustful woman, a forgetful servant and a famine to make sure that the nation of Israel would be protected. And God used that nation, in years to come, to give birth to the one who would provide salvation for all mankind: Jesus Christ.

· Taking It Home ·

1. Are there issues from your past that continue to bring you pain or that cause you problems in your relationships today? Have you been open with someone about these hurtful memories? Do you ever excuse sin in your life because of feeling victimized by the past? How can you allow God to use these difficult situations to bless your life and the lives of others?

2. How did it affect you when you read about the woman who told her daughter who had just been violently raped, "Hating this man is not an option"? How did she show the highest love for her daughter by reminding her of this truth?

3. Joseph's brothers chaffed at the idea of being submissive to their younger brother. How do you react when someone younger than you has some role of authority in your life? Do you easily learn from anyone, or do you have in your mind a certain profile of the type of person you want to learn from?

4. Can you imagine the sense of loneliness Joseph must have felt as the caravan moved slowly away from his home and all that was familiar? Can you imagine the sense of betrayal he felt as his brothers stood by and watched him leave and then didn't change their minds and come after him? Describe the kind of faith he had to have to maintain a positive and giving attitude. What do you need to learn from Joseph?

5. What type of sexual sin are you tempted with? How do you deal with it? How does Joseph encourage you in this area?

6. Joseph remained faithful even when it looked like he had been forgotten. He trusted God and gave his best where he was. (He bloomed where he was planted.) How patient are you as God works out the details and direction of your life?

7. Joseph's brothers did wrong in selling him into slavery, *but God* blessed all of them through it. When you go through difficult situations, do you let them destroy you, or do you say "This bad thing is happening, *but God* is in control and will somehow work for good if I keep trusting him"?

Epilogue

Have you noticed that there are certain places you can visit again and again, and each time you find something new? That's how I feel about the book of Genesis. This most recent journey has taught me more than ever before. It's not because the book has changed, but because I have changed. I am a good bit older than when I sat down in 1975 to read the book for the first time. So much has happened to me since then, both good and bad—but mostly good. God has been out to bless me for the past two decades, even when I wasn't aware of it. That is the message echoing throughout the pages of Genesis: God is out to bless his people.

At times, the men and women of Genesis were aware of his blessings and obeyed wholeheartedly in his presence. At other times, they were oblivious to him and took matters into their own hands. Yet God patiently, tenderly picked them up, brushed them off and used them for his purposes anyway.

We have learned so much from those who lived thousands of years ago. Now is the time to look to ourselves, the disciples of today. We are the "beginning" for a whole new generation of Christian women. Our daughters, granddaughters and those they reach with the gospel will follow us, and they will ask how we have lived the Christian life. If they could study our lives the way we have studied the lives of those in the book of Genesis, what would they see? Would they see women who were frivolously expending their lives in useless pursuits, or women who creatively accomplished their purpose? Would they see women who were deceived by Satan, or women who took a stand for the truth? Would they see women who gave up on devotion to God when things got tough, or women who ran the Christian race to the end? Would they see impatient women who took things into their own hands, or women who trusted until God's promises came true? Would they see women who tore down their homes by their selfish ambition, or women who built up their families by following God's word. Would they see women who put on a phony act, or women who wrestled through their sinful nature to be real with God and others? Would they see women who looked at life from a worldly perspective, or women who looked at their world with the confidence that God was in control?

Sisters, I appeal to you: Join with me in the mission to be true women of God. We are living in an exciting time in the advancement of Christianity. It is a time when history is being made in the kingdom of God. Let us give the next generation an awesome example to follow. Let us be women of faith who will be used by God, no matter what obstacle may come our way.

This journey through the book of Genesis will not be my last. I will return often, each time learning more from the fascinating events that happened thousands of years ago. I will be moved, not just because of the people who lived long ago, but because of the God who still lives. He was there in the beginning, and he is here with me now. He will be with me when I reach the end of this life, and when I start a new beginning with him for eternity.

About the Author

Kay Summers McKean was raised in Miami, Florida, and graduated from the University of Florida in 1975. She and her husband, Randy, have served in the ministry in South Carolina, Florida, Japan and throughout Europe. The McKeans are responsible for mission work in Continental Europe and New England. They currently live in the Boston area with their two teenage children, Summer and Kent, who are also strong disciples of Jesus. In addition to being a devoted wife and mother, Kay is a gifted teacher and writer who shares spiritual insights with clarity and freshness.

The Fine Art of Hospitality

Simply defined, hospitality is the art of sharing your heart and home with others. In this attractively designed book, more than twenty spiritual leaders offer practical, personal and biblical advice in preparing your house, your home and your hearts to draw others into your life and into God's family.

Realizing that hospitality is a lost art in our world, the authors inspire us to become "restorers of the lost art."

Sheila Jones, editor. Hardback, 140 pages.

A companion spiral-bound handbook is divided into two sections: (1) practical tips to better equip you to practice hospitality and (2) tried-and-true recipes for all occasions offered by disciples from around the world. It is designed to be a constant kitchen companion—the type of companion that weathers milk-spills, egg-plops, flour-dustings and becomes dearer with the happy mess of the hospitality process.

Sheila Jones and Betty Dyson, editors. Spiral-bound, 190 pages.

Sold only as a set, $19.99

For more information call
1-888-DPI-BOOK (374-2665)

Or from outside the US
617-938-7396

The Daily Power Series
Series Editors: Thomas and Sheila Jones

Thirty Days at the Foot of the Cross
A study of the central issue of Christianity

First...the Kingdom
A study of the Sermon on the Mount

The Mission
The inspiring task of the church in every generation

Teach Us to Pray
A study of the most vital of all spiritual disciplines

To Live Is Christ
An interactive study of the Letter to the Philippians

Glory in the Church
God's plan to shine through his church

The Heart of a Champion
Spiritual inspiration from Olympic athletes

Jesus with the People
Powerful daily devotionals based on the life of Jesus

Practical Exposition Series

Life to the Full
A study of the writings of James, Peter, John and Jude
by Douglas Jacoby

Mine Eyes Have Seen the Glory
The victory of the Lamb in the Book of Revelation
by Gordon Ferguson

Power in Weakness
Second Corinthians and the Ministry of Paul
by Marty Wooten

The Victory of Surrender
An in-depth study of a powerful biblical concept
(workbook and tapes also available)
by Gordon Ferguson

True and Reasonable
Evidences for God in a skeptical world
by Douglas Jacoby

Raising Awesome Kids in Troubled Times
by Sam and Geri Laing

Friends and Lovers
by Sam and Geri Laing

Let It Shine: A Devotional Book for Teens
edited by Thomas and Sheila Jones

Mind Change: The Overcomer's Handbook
by Thomas A. Jones

She Shall Be Called Woman
Volume I: Old Testament Women
Volume II: New Testament Women
edited by Sheila Jones and Linda Brumley

For information about ordering these
and many other resources from DPI, call
1-888-DPI-BOOK (374-2665)
or from outside the U.S.
617-938-7396
or write to
DPI, One Merrill Street, Woburn, MA 01801-4629
World Wide Web
http://www.dpibooks.com